Mary Virginia Robinson
December 1977.

How to
Live
a
Christian
Life

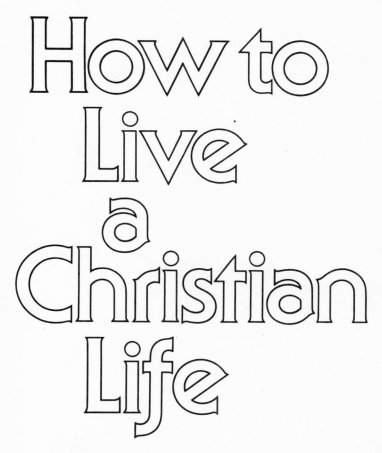

How to Live a Christian Life

CECIL B. MURPHEY

CHRISTIAN HERALD BOOKS
Chappaqua, New York

COPYRIGHT © 1977 by Cecil B. Murphey
First Edition
CHRISTIAN HERALD BOOKS, CHAPPAQUA, NEW YORK 10514
ISBN NO. 0 915684-21-7
LIBRARY OF CONGRESS CATALOG CARD NO. 77-79660

with deepest thanks to
my friends
who have helped

s
h
a
p
e

my life,
but especially
SAM and ANNIE

TABLE OF CONTENTS

MINIMUM DAILY REQUIREMENTS

Rita checked the price of each box she picked up, then flipped it around and read the ingredients.

I smiled to myself, because I'm a label reader, too. I imagined that she read the panel marked "Minimum Daily Requirements." Perhaps she even made a few calculations in her head about whether the family diet met the standards established by the federal government.

She moved on to the canned fish section. I noticed that she held a can of tuna in her hand. Her lips moved slightly as she read the contents.

I picked up a can of Chicken of the Sea tuna and began reading myself:

> The contents of this can supply the following percentages of the U.S. recommended daily allowance of these vitamins and minerals....

They've changed the wording. It's no longer *minimum daily requirements*. Now the labels read *recommended daily allowance*. For me it still means essentially the same—the standard that the federal government believes is essential to maintain good physical health.

As I watched Rita move on down the aisle, I thought, there's a conscientious mother and homemaker. She shops carefully so that her family eats well-balanced meals. From the items in her grocery cart it looks as though she shuns junk food.

At the end of aisle five she paused again and picked up a newly marketed brand of soup. Once again she carefully scrutinized the label. As she stood there, a thought flashed through my mind. I wonder...does God have his recommended daily allowances? Does he have a label which shows the recommended daily allowances (of what?) for healthy Christians?

I dutifully followed my wife Shirley to the end of the aisle and up aisle six. But the thought stayed with me. How much is expected of us by God Himself?

I know I often set my own requirements. I behave as I think a Christian ought to act. But what about God's standards?

Later as I stood in the checkout line, the clerk picked up each item separately and clicked numbers on her cash register. But I kept going back to that disturbing question...What are God's minimum requirements for Christians? Or to ask the same question in another way: What must I do to live a Christian life?

The Bible seems clear enough. But following it doesn't always seem simple.

I don't want to give words of glib assurance that encourage people to assume they are followers of Jesus Christ. However, I don't want to steal the assurance of the godly.

My friend Penney told me about a Sunday school class she taught. She sat with a group of women and the question popped up near the end of the printed lesson material. "How do you know you're a Christian?"

"Well, because I believe in Jesus Christ as my Savior," someone replied very quickly.

"And I believe the Bible, too!" added a second.

"Hmmm, but what if—" someone said half aloud, "What if—if that's not enough."

"Oh, but it is. Believe in the Lord Jesus Christ and you shall be saved. That's right in the Bible. In Acts, I believe," another class member said.

"But—but does that mean," the questioner continued, "that I have to believe all the time? No doubts? I mean, I want to believe. And most of the time I do . . . but. . . ."

"Yes . . . I suppose we all . . . have . . . doubts at times, don't we?" the first person who had been so positive in her assurance replied, weakly.

One by one the others told of their questions. Insecurities. Doubts. Problems that lay people and theologians have been asking for centuries. Martin Luther wrestled continually with the question, "How can a sinful person be made righteous with a holy God?" Eventually he found an answer—by faith. By believing. But even that great father of the Reformation had his periods of doubts and questions, too.

You read portions from Paul's letters and the answer seems simple. *Faith.* That's all you need. But then you read other portions, and you wonder. For example, COLOSSIANS 1:23 concludes, ". . . provided that you continue in the faith, stable and steadfast." Or PHILIPPIANS 2:12, ". . . As you have always obeyed, so now, . . . work out your own salvation with fear and trembling."

And we can't point to our charitable works or our good reputations. Even Jesus said that on the final day of judgment people would appear before him. They would claim they did miracles in his name, that they spread the word of God everywhere. And what would he say? "Get out of here. I never acknowledged you as mine!" (see MATTHEW 7:21-23).

How do I know I'm a Christian? There's no easy answer. But don't let that discourage you. Being a Christian is not a static relationship. We never arrive.

11

We never reach our goal. It's always a matter of moving forward. Of gaining new light. Of striving for a fuller obedience to our God.

Easy solutions give us a false kind of assurance. One person may say, "All I had to do was believe. I confessed Jesus Christ as my Savior twelve years ago." But he may go on to admit that he hasn't shown any spiritual progress in his life since that time. He hasn't conquered his temper. He still doesn't pray or read the Bible. He attends church once a month. He puts a dollar in the offering plate. *But he believes.*

Or another may say, "I'm as good as anyone on my block. I'm a volunteer worker in three civic clubs. I always cook a meal for people when they come home from the hospital. See, look at all the ways I help people. Isn't that enough?" But is that by itself being a *Christian?*

The Apostle Paul wrote, "Therefore, if any one is in Christ, he is a new creation; the old has passed away, behold, the new has come." What does it mean to be a new creation (or creature)? I used to feel that indoctrinating people with the data—the information—of the Christian faith did the trick. Present the gospel in a logical, understandable way, and that will make a person a Christian.

We need information, of course. We need factual material, knowledge of the Bible. We need to memorize the Scriptures so that, as the psalmist says, "I might not sin against Thee." (PSALM 119:11, RSV).

But isn't there something more? Knowing facts alone doesn't make a person a Christian. How can I know—really know—that I'm living a Christian life?

We might ask the question another way: Who exactly are the Christians today, the ones fulfilling God's minimum daily requirement for spiritual well-being?

First, we really can't answer that question. God

12

doesn't call on us to decide who has entered into his kingdom. We do have hints, of course. A person's lifestyle and attitude may make us dubious of his faith. But only God really knows the heart. And the final decision is His alone.

Second, we have enough to do to make ourselves more like Jesus Christ without asking about the faith of others. We are called to wrestle with our own particular problems, to show growth in our commitment to Christ, to meet the "minimum daily requirements" ourselves.

Third, there's no easy answer. There's nothing so absolutely objective that we can say, "See, this proves I'm a Christian." Our own sense of faith in Jesus Christ is surely important. But what about our obedience to his commandments? What about those who almost-but-not-quite obey? What about our own record of being unfaithful sometimes?

Jesus put this question in several different ways. The most suggestive allusion is in his famous parable of the sheep and the goats. He said the sheep were those who helped people, those who fulfilled the ministry of compassion that God had called them to. The goats ignored the needs, closed their eyes. And the Lord will say to the goats, "Depart from me. . ." (MATTHEW 25:41).

The Sermon on the Mount (MATTHEW 5-7) gives a pretty good view of the Christian experience. It centers around the question "How can I know—really know—that I'm a Christian?" Being a Christian is not absorbing a lot of information. Nor is it following a list of rules, or memorizing laws. The Christian life begins with a spontaneous response to God's love. And that response can be summed up in what Jesus called the first and second commandments: Love God with your whole being and then your neighbor as yourself.

Not loving God only. Not only loving your neighbor.

13

But God first and then other human beings along with a healthy love for ourselves.

Jesus' teaching in Matthew 6 focuses on that first and great commandment of loving God above all else. Although Jesus never separates our relationship with him from our relationship to other people, this chapter stresses first our right standing with God himself.

In Matthew 6:1-18 Jesus calls for our complete devotion to God our Father. In the rest of chapter 6 he urges us to trust in a Father who, despite all outward circumstances, still cares about us. The first part of Matthew 7 emphasizes the other perspective: Our relationship to people. Attitudes and actions toward other human beings seem good indicators of our relationship to God. Do we judge others? Find ourselves eager to correct them? Treat them lovingly?

Our response to people, however, doesn't answer the ultimate question. It's not what they think of us or how they respond to us. Not even how we treat them. While the quality of our human relationships are good indicators of Christian commitment God alone ultimately decides who is truly a Christian. It's what he thinks of us that matters most. He's the one who sets up the daily minimum requirements of faith. And he's the one who knows whether we meet those requirements or not. That's the theme of the rest of Matthew 7.

I won't say, read this book and learn everything you need to know about how to live successfully as a Christian. But I hope the book will buttress your commitment to know and follow Jesus Christ. And I wouldn't want you to be satisfied merely with meeting the *minimum* standards. But it's an awfully good starting place, isn't it?

Beware of practicing your religious duties [or righteousness] in public in order to be seen by them. If you do these things publicly you won't have a reward from your heavenly Father.

MATTHEW 6:1 TEV

GRAB IT NOW OR GET IT LATER

"Sometimes I want to stop helping people," Helen moaned.

"I know how you feel. People are so thankless," replied Harriett.

"Why, look at the people outside our church that we've helped! We've provided clothing, food money, furniture—and what good has it done? Have any of them ever joined our church or even come around to express their appreciation?"

"I get discouraged helping, too," Minnie added. "In the twenty-seven years I've been a member here, I've taken food to the sick, given more than a tenth of my income to the church. I've organized women to go to homes and sweep, wash, and iron. I have personally spent hundreds of hours in hospitals and sick rooms. If anyone has even needed anything, I've tried to be there."

"That's probably right," timidly spoke up Janet Wayne. "But...if you had received your full reward on earth, you wouldn't have anything waiting for you in eternity, would you?"

Janet may have spoken too bluntly, but her words hit

15

home to at least two of the women present. She was paraphrasing the warning of Jesus not to do your religious duties in public so people will see what you do.

If we help people merely to be seen and appreciated, then we have our reward. People's smiles, words of appreciation, or our reputation for kindness pays us in full.

Jesus spoke of a doing that has no idea of reward or human appreciation involved. He taught us to do what is loving and kind but to do it to glorify the Father in heaven and not just to receive commendations from people.

Some people have assumed that this command by Jesus flatly contradicts his earlier statement, "Let your light so shine before men, that they may see your good works and give glory to your Father who is in heaven" (MATTHEW 5:16 RSV). Now Jesus says, "Beware of practicing your righteousness in public in order to be seen by them."

We read these two statements, scratch our heads, and ask, "What are we supposed to do? On the one hand, we're to go out of our way and show people that we're serving Jesus Christ and then here we're told to hide what we're doing."

That's the paradox. It's like many we face in our struggle to lead a balanced Christian life. If we obey God by shutting ourselves away in a secret place or working only anonymously, then we're not being seen by people. Then how will they know it's a follower of God doing it?

There's no real contradiction. We can do *both*! Our primary purpose in life is to glorify God in everything. But do it without ostentation! Without calling attention to ourselves. Without making certain that everyone knows of our contribution. Our actions will glorify our Father. We don't have to do them in secret, for fear of someone else finding out.

Someone helped me once by saying, "Show you're tempted to hide, but hide when you're tempted to show."

Then we'll not have to worry about rewards from God.

Rewards? "Doesn't that sound a bit mercenary?" a deacon once asked me. "I mean, as Christians we love God. We give our time, talents, and service as a privilege. To expect rewards...seems calculating, un-spiritual."

"Isn't the reward of the Christian life the good life itself?" Dennis asked. "For half a century Christ has been my Lord. It's been a wonderful life. The blessings of God from day to day satisfy me."

Rewards trouble Christians. We attempt to live exemplary, obedient lives. Shouldn't that end the matter? We do a kindly act and feel satisfied, knowing we took the right step. Isn't it below Christian dignity to think of anything beyond?

Yet the commission of the good act doesn't end it all. God prepares future rewards and blessings for His people. Jesus taught both the importance and certainty of rewards. The Beatitudes promise happiness because of our poverty in spirit...our making peace...enduring persecution. In another place the Lord states that anyone giving a cup of cold water in his name will not lose his reward (MATTHEW 25:35). The parable of the talents points out that faithfulness merits recognition and reward in the end (MATTHEW 25:14-30).

The Old Testament strongly supports the idea of reward and punishment. If people obey God and treat their fellow human beings properly, they flourish.

Their crops increase, and prosperity exists. But the indolent and wicked find only hard times and poverty.

Job's friends recognized the principle that God blesses good and despises evil. All they understood of Job's ordeal was his affliction, which to them meant the disfavor of God. These friends of Job had a naive view of life, as did many of their contemporaries. Centuries passed before people were able to go beyond that concept of immediate retribution for wrongdoing.

But during the 400-year span of time between the last book of the Old Testament and the first of the New Testament writings, a strange thing happened. Good Jews suffered martyrdom. Faithful disciples of God experienced defeat, exile, and even death. Conscientious Jews asked questions and demanded answers. People also suffer for doing *right!* What happens then? This thought eventually permeated and troubled the Jewish mind.

The Old Testament book of Habakkuk raises the question of suffering at the hands of the wicked. The Jewish people had done wickedly themselves. They had disobeyed the commandments of God and turned to strange forms of worship. They could see why God would punish them. But to use the Chaldeans—a nation far more wicked—as his instrument? Habakkuk acknowledges God's purity and then asks, "We are wicked, but they far more! Will you stand idly by while they swallow us up? Should you be silent while the wicked destroy those who are better than they?" (HABAKKUK 1:13 LIVING BIBLE).

The book ends on a note of faith. "I don't understand it all, but I accept it, even though everything goes wrong and nothing comes out right for me." The prophet concludes, "Yet I will rejoice in the Lord, I will joy in the God of my salvation" (HABAKKUK 3:18 RSV).

18

The Jews knew that a day of reckoning would come. In the final stage of life—sometime when the scales would be properly weighed, rewards and punishments would be meted out to all people. Doesn't logic tell us this must be so? To banish rewards from religion says that injustice declares the final verdict. The end of all men—good and bad alike—becomes the same.

"Sure, but doesn't that create problems?" queried Steve. "Even believing in rewards isn't enough. Doing things in order to get blessed by God? That doesn't seem right."

Harry spoke up. "I remember my high school days. The 'in group' of our school worked hard to say the 'right' words. They were fakes and most of us knew it. Always the 'nice' people. Complimenting everyone. Fawning over everything. They only wanted to be popular. Somehow members of that group were elected to all of the important school positions. That's what they worked for. Does God want us to be like that?"

"No," I replied, "Jesus never speaks *against* rewards, but he teaches about the various kinds of rewards. People get what they bargain for. They grab it now or they get it later. We aim for popularity at the expense of integrity. Or we can put principles first—and that might gain us temporary disfavor. We're human. We all need approval and acceptance for our actions. One way to get approval is to say, 'Look at the work I've accomplished! See my embroidered tablecloth. My homemade jet engine. My beautiful paint work in the kitchen. My "A" on the final exam in English class.'

"That's one way. Another is doing something because you enjoy doing it. Or because you see a need. Or because you care. You don't look for a reward but you end up with a good feeling inside. It's the kind of feeling that makes you know Jesus Christ approves. Perhaps even the kind that one day will cause him to say, 'Well done, good and faithful servant.'"

Barbara exemplifies this second kind of attitude. When sickness strikes, she's the first to visit or to comfort the bereaved. She's been the shoulder to lean on many times. She always has a listening ear. She enjoys loving people. Yet all her good deeds have been reported to me by someone else!

But how often we find subtle ways of telling others what we've done. Homer stopped in at the office the other day. "I went to see Johnny Patterson in the hospital. He certainly appreciated my visit. And he liked the fruit basket even better than the flowers I took the other day." Homer conveyed information. But he was also telling me, "Look at my Good Samaritan spirit!"

I'm not much like Barbara. And I'm usually not so blatant as Homer. But there's an element in me that keeps grabbing for immediate appreciation from people. When I've helped someone, my inner self cries out for recognition. But I'm also learning that the satisfaction of helping another person is a reward in itself. Like the smile and mumbled words of thanks when I helped Darrell get a job. Or the hug from Margie for rushing over when we heard about the death of her only brother.

Doing the deed and looking for nothing beyond— God surely approves! That means no need to tell people how wonderful I am. Or how kind. Or thoughtful. I know how, in subtle ways, those things keep sneaking out. And I'm still fighting it! Frankly, it's still difficult not to let people know that yesterday I went three miles out of my way to offer a man a ride to church. Or that we decided *not* to buy a new car this year in order to give more to foreign missions. Friends may approve my actions if I tell them. Perhaps even admire my dedication. But it makes me wonder where I stand with Jesus Christ.

Two questions have helped in my own dilemma. They force me to evaluate my motives and my actions.

1. Why am I doing it? If I calculate the benefit either to the recipient or to myself, I may be missing out on God's approval.

Maria attended our church for about three months. During that time I saw her wear only two different dresses. Her husband, ill with cancer, had been hospitalized for months and with a daughter also to care for, she couldn't work. From friends I received several dresses, coats, blouses and skirts and joyfully carried them to her house. In my mind, visions of happiness surrounded the act. I pictured her great burst of enthusiasm and lavish praise.

As I handed them to her, she took them, saying nothing for a long time. Finally she asked with a clear trace of her Cuban accent, "Why did you bring these to me? Am I so poor or so sloppy? Because we came to this country as refugees, are we always despised? Are my dresses not clean? If I came without a washed dress or with dirty spots, I could accept these. I don't have many clothes...but I don't want charity either."

Dumbstruck, I scarcely knew how to respond. Why *had* we collected these things? Then I knew. "I'm sorry I offended you, Ma'am. These clothes came to me from a few friends who care about you. We had no wish to embarrass or humiliate. Our purpose was to share. I'm sorry." "Ah, well," her eyes sparkled, "in that case, I accept. To offer from concern is good, is it not? My thanks to all of you."

2. What's the best way to do it? As favor to a vacationing pastor I agreed to preach in a small church for a mid-week service. On the way, the car broke down, taking most of my cash for repairs. The church gave me no honorarium for the service. There was only enough gas in the car to get half-way home. I drove a few miles down the road, feeling sorry for Cec Murphey. I put my hand in my coat pocket. As I pulled it out, I found a ten dollar bill rolled up in a piece of paper. The note said, "I felt God wanted me to share this money with you."

How did the money get there? Or when? I have no idea. That donor will never know the importance of that anonymous gift. But God knows! His knowledge is even more important than the donor's personal satisfaction.

It's difficult for me to let my righteousness show only to God. It's easier to display my spirituality and dedication. But Jesus cautions, "Beware of practicing your piety before people in order to be seen by them." Working primarily to please God—that's one of the growing edges of my life. And growing in that area is one of the ways that I know *internally* that I'm a Christian. I'm learning more and more to be satisfied with the joy of knowing I've helped another human being. That I've done it without ostentation.

And even that sometimes I haven't even been thanked. *But God knows*. And when I don't get the smile or the "thank you," I still get the Lord's approval. And that's part of what it means to be a Christian!

3

Whenever you give anything to the poor, don't blow a trumpet, as the hypocrites do in the places of worship and in the streets. They do that in order to be recognized and praised. Remember this! They have already been paid in full. But you, when you see a needy person, help in such a way that even your left hand won't know what your right hand is doing. Let your charitable deeds be in secret and your Father who sees that you do in secret, will openly reward you.

MATTHEW 6:2-4 TEV

GIVING IT GOD'S WAY

There's an Enid in every church, civic organization, and community.

At the PTA bake sale all her goodies have a plastic tape bearing these words, "donated by Enid Rogers."

She persuaded Carrie to borrow her green scarf because "it sets off your suit so well." At the wedding, Enid commented, "Doesn't Carrie look lovely in that suit? Don't you think my scarf just puts on the finishing touch?" People usually agree. In such circumstances, good manners prevent a negative reply. And Enid feels contented. She has given to someone else.

In the last chapter I wrote about rewards. God rewards giving—when done in the right way.

Jesus also sounded a warning, "When you give alms, don't sound a trumpet." This allegorical expression means, "Don't tell everyone the good you're going." If you're lending, do it quietly. If donating, do it unobtrusively. Some people give as though they expect a trumpet to blow or a bell to ring. They constantly distribute for the effect it creates. Or for the attention received.

The giving of alms, for the Jews, was so important that they considered it the highest act of goodness. The Hebrew word for alms can be translated two different ways: *righteousness* or *almsgiving*. The Jewish mind saw no more positive indication of piety than in attitudes toward the poor. The godly looked at needs about them, doing whatever they could.

Almsgiving extended beyond the tithe (tenth) required by Mosaic law. Assisting the poor came after their obligations had been met in giving to God. The principle which Jesus lays down about giving to the needy, however, applies to all kinds of contributions.

He also warned against giving for the wrong reasons. One of those is to receive the praises of people.

Frank and Evelyn became active members of a social organization in their community. For six years they sacrificed themselves. Anything to be done: call the Barlows. Last year Frank was elected state chairman. He and Evelyn faced the task of preparing for the annual three-day convention. The couple expended uncounted time and energy, accumulating gray hairs and frayed nerves. Everything went smoothly because Frank and Evelyn planned well. On the final day of the convention, the speaker remarked (and it appeared more as an afterthought), "And, of course, thanks to the folks in this city who hosted the convention."

Later Evelyn fumed. "I lived on aspirin and coffee two weeks and slept less than four hours a night. I never had time to enjoy a single meeting. What happens? Not even thanks to us by name. Not even the courtesy to call us out of the crowd. Just a kind of P.S. acknowledgment." Frank resigned from the organization. Both have refused to attend meetings or participate since.

Someone slipped up. Courtesy would, of course, demand a recognition of work well done. It also becomes obvious why Frank and Evelyn worked tirelessly. They worked for appreciation, for prestige, for thanks. When denied approval and recognition, they resigned. They exemplify the wrong kind of giving. This attitude looks at tasks in terms of ultimate receipts. "If I do this...I'll get this in return."

How many times have you heard people ask, "What's in it for me?" We may not consciously speak this way. Yet our actions and attitudes tell the truth. I often encounter people who leave positions or refuse to serve again. "It's a thankless job," replied one Sunday School teacher. "I'm tired of all the complaining. If a speck of dirt appears or a dish gets broken, *I* get all the back-talk!" moaned the church's kitchen chairman.

Maybe that's the most wonderful place to be! Just think: a place of service where only God appreciates your efforts. And where only God can provide rewards. That's the right kind of giving.

Another kind of giving stems from duty or compulsion. Ever wonder why charitable organizations send people knocking on doors? Most of us don't know how to say a blunt "no." It's easier to slap down a dollar and close the door. We don't want to be known as tightwads. We abhor the idea that others in the neighborhood will think of us as the family who refused to contribute.

Why do we pass the offering plate, from row to row each Sunday? Money can be as easily deposited in a box at the rear of the sanctuary. I'm not sure of all the reasons, but it's good psychology.

Long before I stood on my side of the pulpit, I sat in many pews. The inevitable offering plates passed me every service. Eventually it occurred to me that no matter how little money I had, or how bountifully I had contributed at the previous service, that offering plate intimidated me. The combination of an offering plate, and ushers at both ends of the pew, made me feel almost as if I had sinned against the Lord until I made my contribution.

There are churches in which the psychology of the offering works even more effectively. In one such church in Wisconsin every Sunday the pianist plays a militant-sounding offertory. Two large plates rest on the communion table. Each person stands, marches to the front and drops in his/her contributions. Rarely does an adult pass by without at least a token offering. The pastor beamed, "Our offerings have increased 31% since we began this system!"

Pressure. Obligation. Guilt. These factors work. Results abound. But one thing they don't do: they don't instill joyfulness. Or the sense of pleasing God by the gift.

Another subtle pressure: "What will people say?" During my military days, our chief petty officer came around collecting money for Navy Relief. Janette, a Wave, sat at the desk across from me. When asked for a contribution she replied, "No, thanks, not this year."

"You don't have to give a lot."

She shook her head.

The officer smiled slightly and replied evenly, "We're out to make this department rate 100%. That means everyone making a contribution. So far, everyone has donated except you."

He rattled the cigar box in which the contributions

had been placed. "Put something in the box and then sign your name on the paper."

"No, thank you," Janette replied again, returning to work.

The man persisted. "What kind of religious person are you? Always talking about love and helping people? Navy Relief does a lot of good."

"I'm not arguing against Navy Relief. I'm simply choosing not to make a contribution."

"Here I stand, asking for a dollar. Even fifty cents. And you refuse! You're really some Christian!"

Janette smiled. "I choose not to give. Like everyone else in the military, my money comes in limited quantities. Besides my own church I contribute to the Red Cross and the Salvation Army. You have no right to force me into giving to the Navy Relief. Even if it's only a dime."

As I put my dollar in the box, I secretly applauded Janette. She gave with the right kind of spirit—and withheld with integrity! She refused to let public opinion, or the derogatory remarks or our chief petty officer, intimidate her.

Some think presenting a gift in secret makes the motive right. Secret giving in itself may be just as wrong as publicly heralding with great ostentation. An anonymous contribution can be as proudly thought of by the donor. Jesus said, "Don't let the right hand know what the left hand is doing." A clever fellow added, "and don't tell the head either!" Giving secretly can be as pride-inducing as any other method. If I present an anonymous gift, what motivates me? Material to mark up in my private ledger? Added score to the blessings being stored up in heaven? Forget it! With that spirit, my self-satisfaction has already been paid in full!

There are right ways of giving. When it originates

from the inner self, when concern for another's needs stir us. When a contribution arises spontaneously without question of return. Giving from gratitude to God should rank high on the list. Our youth group used to sing a chorus which I recall went in part: "How can I do less than give him my best, after all He's done for me?"

Blanche Stuart labored in the same area of Kenya where we did. Her predecessor had been a woman of private and extensive means and had lavished gifts freely on the national workers. Blanche never attempted to compete. She offered no inducements to service. Blanche worked tirelessly in her training programs. At the end of a four-year stint, she returned to her native Australia. Amoebic dysentery had sapped her strength by infecting her liver. A group of national women's leaders came to say good-bye. They brought small gifts of food and embroidery work. One woman handed Blanche seven shillings she had earned by selling fish for ten hours in the market (the amount was about $1.00 in American money). Blanche bade them a tearful farewell. "You've been so kind and loving toward me. I'm genuinely touched. You have so little and have given so much. I regret I have little to share with you." Uma spoke up, "Little? You think the other teacher before you loved us more because she gave us so much? She gave us gifts: clothes, money, books. For that we have been grateful. You gave us more: you have loved us!"

That's the giving which pleases Jesus Christ. That kind of giving flows out of a loving heart. It is another mark of living a Christian life.

*And when you pray, don't be like show-offs!
They love to stand up and pray in the places
of worship and on the street corners in order
that everyone may see them. Remember this!
They have already been paid in full. But
when you pray, go into your room, close the
door, and pray to your Father who is
unseen. And your Father, who sees what you
do in private, will reward you.*

MATTHEW 6:5-6 TEV

WHEN *YOU* PRAY

Did you hear the gong? It's nine o'clock in the morning.
Nothing of importance to you perhaps. But to an
orthodox Jew of Jesus' day that particular hour held a
special meaning. It was one of the three set times of
daily prayer. Again at exactly noon. Then at three in
the afternoon.

The Jews were a praying people. Communion with
God held a place of high esteem in their lives. They
repeated two set prayers every day. First, the *Shema*.
This comes from the Hebrew word *hear* and is the first
word of the commandment in Deuteronomy 6:4,
"Hear, O Israel: The Lord our God is one Lord." The
actual *shema* prayed was a little longer—Deuteronomy
6:4-9 and 11:13-21, and Numbers 15:37-41. Every
faithful Jew repeated the *shema* as early as possible
every morning, and certainly no later than nine
o'clock. It had to be said again by nine in the evening.

A second daily prayer for every Jew was the *Shemoneh esreh* or *The Eighteen*. Originally it consisted of eighteen prayers and is still an integral part of synagogue services. The rabbis expected the faithful to repeat these formal prayers three times a day. There was a summary which a man might pray if he didn't have time to repeat the entire eighteen. And for many the prayers became nothing more than a ritual of the past with little real significance.

This didn't end the prayer life of the Hebrew people. They had prayers for every occasion—a prayer before eating, another after the meal, a prayer after receiving good news, one for going on a journey. Seemingly, every occasion had a formal prayer.

What a grand intention—to bring everything into the presence of God. It was a way of saying that nothing is too insignificant to involve God.

But that very concept also presented problems. Because prayers were so meticulously prescribed, the practice easily led to formalism. And prayers tended to slip off the tongue with little meaning. Rabbis often warned against this glibness of prayer, but the danger was always present.

So, as so often happens in life, over a period of time many Jews took God's fellowship for granted. Or some merely went through their duties with little grasp of the words. Prayer often became merely a duty.

Another problem: religious practices made ostentacious prayer easy. A praying Jew stood with head bowed and stretched out his arms with palms upwards. For orthodox Jews, in the days of the first century, prayer went on three times daily. Wherever a man found himself at those set times, he stopped to pray. How easy to suddenly find oneself on a busy street corner or in a crowded marketplace at the set time of prayer. A pious Jew could then lengthily and demonstratively offer prayers to God for all less religious people to observe.

Jesus directed true disciples otherwise! "People don't have to know that you pray. God knows—and after all, isn't He the one who really matters?"

Tom joined the church where I was pastor. Prayer had not been a significant part of his life. "I guess I never thought about it before," he said to me. A few weeks later he told me of an incident at work. Every day he went out to the parking lot after eating lunch, and sat down under an old oak tree. He leaned his head against the trunk of the tree and closed his eyes. The guard watched him every day. At first he had suspected Tom of stealing from the company and taking the goods to his car. But Tom never went close to any parked cars. By the middle of the second week, his curiosity was really roused. He followed Tom.

"I've seen you come out here every single work day. Even on days when it's not particularly good weather. The other men stay inside and talk, or play cards, or nap in a corner. You come out here all by yourself and just sit. Hey, what are you doing? Praying or something?"

Tom looked at the guard and replied, "As a matter of fact, I have been praying."

"You're putting me on!"

"I can't find a place at home because we're so rushed, always so much noise. But each day I like to come out here for a while. I can get alone with God. Nothing to distract me."

Tom practiced the suggestion Jesus made about prayer. He said go into a private place and pray. Don't advertise. Just do it. Pray! But pray for God's ears and eyes.

Shortly after my conversion I joined a church.

31

There I learned one important lesson: they stressed private prayer. Our Sunday school class of young adults seemed to judge people in terms of how long they prayed or even whether they prayed privately each day. I learned to use prayer as a test of orthodoxy. Spiritual people not only set aside a *minimum* of thirty minutes daily for prayer; they would say, "The other day, when I was having my devotions. . . ," or, "Before I began living the Spirit-filled life and setting aside daily time. . . ."

Jesus taught, "Don't make a show of prayer. Prayer is secret. Not for sharing with someone else, but for you and God only."

He instructed us to hide away—to go to a place where we can be alone. It doesn't matter where. Under a shade tree, like Tom. In the quiet of the living room before the rest of the family gets up. One man I know gets up at six o'clock every morning and walks and prays for thirty minutes. Kelly spends his thirty-seven minutes of driving time to work in fellowship with Jesus Christ. Secret places? They're everywhere. We can find them if we look.

One summer I traveled with a quartet, representing a denominational college. Mostly we stayed in hotels and were in each other's company twenty-four hours a day. Some days I found my secret place riding alongside the other young men. On other days, I shut myself in the bathroom after they had gone to bed. Any place can be a secret place with Jesus!

When we go into that closed "room," we need to acknowledge that not only is prayer secret but it's also private. God and me. I have times for prayer with my wife and with my children. Or in sharing groups. Or in public worship. But the most important time, I feel, is the time I spend alone with Jesus.

I like to think of my meeting with God as a trysting place. It is a place where lovers meet; we need share with no one else. I talk to him about other people, but it is an intimate conversation. Prayer is also personal. The words are for the ears of Jesus Christ alone.

During my military days, a Christian young man joined our fellowship. Wayne kept looking for a place to get alone with God for prayer. He played trumpet in the military band, the hours were long, and he had no private place to get away. One day he discovered an anteroom at the side of the chapel. The chapel and the room were kept open twenty-four hours a day. Wayne made it his habit to go there every evening immediately after the supper hour. Wayne didn't have to tell us he was praying! It was only too obvious to everyone. To reach my barracks I had to walk behind the chapel. I could hear his voice screaming out as if in agony. The first time I almost burst in, fearing he had suffered a heart attack. He was only praying.

I don't want to judge Wayne. After all, what's wrong with shouting to God? But I often wondered if he really sought the secret place? He might have been unconscious of the noise he made. Or perhaps, in his way, Wayne was broadcasting his spirituality.

Another significant fact about prayer: it's God-centered, the prayer of a child talking to its heavenly Father. It's fellowship between the creature and the Creator. No need to concentrate on grammar, length of time, or aptness of expression. We're talking to our Lord who understands us completely.

Prayer is still God-directed and God-centered when prayed audibly. As a minister, I find this hard to remember. In public worship, prayer is still for his ears. The most distressing compliment I receive is, "You pray such beautiful prayers." While I understand the

33

intent, the real compliment is when I see moist eyes. Or sense changed attitudes. Or when I'm aware that I'm in close fellowship with the Lord. I constantly have to guard against praying for the ears of others.

During my college days I went out with my pastor as part of our church's visitation program. A man with much zeal, he never lost an opportunity to speak up for Jesus Christ—even if he overstepped the bounds of propriety. On one occasion he attempted to talk to a couple about the Lord. Mostly they shrugged their shoulders. An occasional "Naw" or "Yeah." He tried asking about their religious beliefs. Nothing but a blank stare from both.

"Are you church members?"

"Nope. We're not very religious, preacher."

Not to be outdone, the minister tried once more. "May I pray with you before I leave?"

"Uh, guess so."

"Dear God and Loving Father," he began, "We give you thanks for the gift of eternal life which is found only in and through Jesus Christ your son. In him and only in him is there eternal life for all of us sinners, for we know that your word declares that God so loved the world that he gave. . . ."

The prayer wound endlessly down the passageway of every evangelistic scripture my pastor could recall. In my agony and embarrassment I felt he would never stop. The couple had been taken advantage of—regardless of how noble the cause. Trapped. We never saw them in our church. I'm not sure his "evangelistic prayer" helped much.

What concerned me most of all, was the purely horizontal direction of that prayer: he didn't talk to God, so far as I could discern. He used his prayer to speak to people. He kept saying, "Loving God" or "Heavenly Father" but directed his words toward the couple.

34

Jesus taught a second lesson about effective praying:

*In your prayers don't use a lot of words, as
the pagans do. They think God hears
because of their lengthy prayers. Don't
imitate them. God is your father. He already
knows what you need before you ask him.*

(MATTHEW 6:7-8, my own translation).

The length of your prayers has nothing to do with spirituality. Right motives and right attitudes gain the Father's ear! Peter cried one of the most desperate and sincere prayers in the Bible—and one of the short-est!—"Lord, we perish!" It got results: Jesus calmed the stormy sea.

Somehow, some people have equated length with quality! They may have gotten their inspiration from the contest between Elijah and the prophets of Baal. The issue revolved around who was the true God—the Lord of the Hebrews or Baal. The 450 prophets of Baal offered a sacrifice, laid it on the altar and waited for Baal to burn it up. They prayed. They pleaded. They cried out to God. From morning until noon they prayed (see I KINGS 18:25-26). No answer.

Watching from the sidelines, Elijah jeered them. They prayed again. They kept crying out, cutting themselves with swords and knives. Blood gushed from their arms and legs. They prayed all through that afternoon, until sundown, at the time of the evening offerings. "But there was no voice; no one answered, no one heeded" (I KINGS 18:29).

They illustrate the negative side of Jesus' principle: they could not bribe God . . . either by length of peti-tions, high-sounding words or repetition of requests.

Then Elijah prayed and, almost instantaneously, fire from heaven licked up the offering.

We can smugly think of the heathen, fold our arms

and murmur, "Ah, yes, pagans." We know better than that. We never use 'vain repetitions.' Even though we may get caught up in a continuous strain of "bless John, bless Alice, bless Terry. . . ."

I wonder how many times our minds concentrate on the Lord's Prayer when we say it? How many times do we sincerely give thanks to God when we pray, "Lord, for this food. . . ." Do we really know what we say when we say, "Forgive our many sins?"

Any words prayed without comprehension can become a vain repetition. That includes mechanical praying. That includes mumbling words without meaning them.

In an informal gathering, a teenager was asked to lead in prayer. He started, "For this food, Lord, we thank—" paused slightly, realizing what he had said, recovered quickly and added, "you—yes, Lord, for this spiritual food which we will feast on tonight." The difference between him and some of the praying we've all done—and that includes me—is that we keep on saying the words, but have long lost the meaning.

Agnes once complained about her husband, "When he starts to pray at our devotions, I know every word he's going to say. He prays exactly the same way every day and has been praying that way for more than forty years. I wonder if his mind is even on what he's saying to the Lord."

For me, part of being a Christian means setting aside time for Jesus Christ. Just the two of us. A time when we share like two close friends. A time when I receive new strength for my tasks, or guidance for the responsibilities. A time when he assures me he loves me. I know I belong to Jesus Christ; I'm one of his people.

5

*"In your prayers do not use a lot of meaningless
words, as the pagans do, who think that God will
hear them because of their long prayers. Do not be
like them; your Father already knows what you
need before you ask him. This, then, is how you
should pray:
'Our Father in heaven:
May your holy name be honored;
may your Kingdom come;
may your will be done on earth as it is in heaven.
Give us today the food we need;
Forgive us the wrongs that we have done as we
forgive the wrongs that have been done us.
Do not bring us to hard testing, but keep us safe
from the Evil One.'"*

MATTHEW 6:7-13 TEV

IMITATORS AND IMPROVISORS

Want a more invigorating prayer life? Why not go
directly to the expert—to Jesus himself!

Jesus gave the disciples a formula prayer—a prayer
to be imitated.

But before giving the words of the sample prayer,
Jesus gave them instructions.

First, how *not* to pray. Don't pray to show off; don't
direct your words to people's ears—you're talking to
God himself, so when you pray aim your words for his
hearing.

Jesus criticizes repetition. The Greek word Matthew

37

uses for "repetition" literally means "to babble." It means to pray like the priests of Baal who howled and wept and repeated their prayers over and over (I KINGS 18:22-4). Christians can pray like that. I attended a meeting once in which a woman repeated the word "Jesus" over and over again.

Now repetition itself isn't wrong—even Jesus prayed the same prayer several times in the garden. But he teaches against unthinking repetition, of letting words go through your lips without letting them first go through your head.

Twenty-four hour prayer chains can be criticized, too. The Jews picked up lengthy prayers quite naturally. In the Old Testament there are a number of long prayers (see DANIEL 9:4-19 or II CHRONICLES 6:14-42). When Jesus spoke of repetition he probably had in mind the three daily prayers in which pious Jews offered eighteen petitions—each of them longer than the model prayer he taught.

True prayer isn't long words or erudite phrases. It's prayer which comes from the heart, meant only for the ears of God.

According to Jesus, God doesn't need to be informed of all our needs, as though he were unconscious or needed reminding or wheeling into action. Years ago we used to attend a regular prayer service in which one elderly lady always prayed. And prayed. And prayed. Her favorite words were, "And, Lord, thou knowest that. . . ." and she told the Lord about Harold's need for a job and explained carefully why he had lost it and why it was important for him to have a new one immediately. She went into detail about Anne's chronic kidney dysfunction. If God knows, why tell him in such detail?

Jesus also taught positively. When you do pray, hide

away from the world; get alone by yourself and God will be more real. He gave his disciples a brief prayer which they probably used in their own daily worship. The prayer itself is largely a summary of Jewish piety. Most of the phrases and expressions were already in use. Jesus streamlined the lengthy petitions and stated them succinctly for the people.

I've been told that many great painters learned their craft by studying the masters. They diligently copied Leonardo, Rembrandt, van Gogh. When you learn you use the best possible model. Why learn by copying the methods of a second-rate teacher?

I started writing by taking a course under Charlie Shedd. He's a prolific author. His book *Letters to Karen* was condensed by *Reader's Digest* and has sold over a million copies. I've lost track of the number of books, articles, and columns for newspapers and magazines that Charlie has put out. He's not only a selling writer—but a top pro.

When I first began writing, I slavishly followed every rule Charlie laid down. "No sentence more than fifteen words" was the rule. For at least a year I counted words in every sentence that looked as though it might exceed the limit. I ruthlessly cut them down, slashing one word, ten words, or breaking a long sentence into two shorter sentences.

I no longer count words. I've grown beyond that elementary rule. But it helped in the beginning. When Charlie gave me that rule, I looked at an article over which I had worked and worked. It looked fine. The article ought to sell. It was almost a masterpiece! Then I counted the words in my opening sentence: *one hundred and three.* Before that article ever got into an editor's hands, that sentence became four sentences.

I learned to improvise on his rules. Sometimes a

sentence contains sixteen words. Or even thirty. Then a sentence follows with only five. Or two.

That's what I believe Jesus meant in giving us his model prayer. Improvise.

By improvise, I don't mean improve. How can we improve on the perfect formula Jesus gave us? He laid out all the basics of prayer.

Look at the divisions of the prayer. The first section (verses 9-10) He devotes to God: praise, worship, petition for the kingdom of heaven. The second section (verses 11-13) concerns humanity; ourselves and our fellows. Any concern, any burden, any problem fits under one of those categories. Jesus gave the basic formula. He wants us to improvise.

I see the Lord's prayer as though Jesus said to his disciples, "You don't know *how* to pray? Or is it that you don't know *what* to pray? Try this for a starter: Our Father in heaven. . . ."

If we need to follow that pattern for a period of time, that's fine. But somewhere along the line we should begin to improvise and make the prayer our own. Individual. Personal. It becomes *my* praying.

The real idea of improvising means to adapt or change without planning or premeditation. We pray the formula prayer of Jesus. It sinks into our hearts, our unconscious self. One day it comes out through our own thought patterns. We develop our individual methods of expressing concerns.

Ever compare the Lord's prayer as recorded by Matthew and Luke? Luke gives a far shorter version. Neither one of them records, "For thine is the kingdom and the power and the glory forever." Most scholars see this as a clear reference to I Chronicles 29:11-13, in which David blesses the people shortly before his death. So far as we can tell, the church before the beginning of the second century added this to the formula prayer. They could do it because they grasped the *spirit* of the prayer.

But how do we improvise the Lord's prayer? Think about the prayer itself. First we focus on God. I wonder if we don't make our big mistake there! Our tendency in praying is to think about ourselves: our needs, our world, our burdens. Jesus started with the Father. He recognized the one to whom He prayed. We start by talking to the Maker of Heaven and Earth. He's greater than the needs of all the people in the world combined. Many of us *start* there. "Heavenly Father, thank you for . . ." and then a hurried trek on to the "real matter" of prayer.

How do I know? I've done the same thing myself! Often. Much of the opening part of my prayer has sounded like the preface of a book. Not a terribly vital part. A quick introduction. For years I have struggled over this. My tendency is to make God only the preface.

How much of our praying centers on the holiness of God? The extension of his vast kingdom? His will being done on heaven and earth? We might be concerned about the kingdom or about his will—but often only in terms of our immediate needs.

One lesson I'm learning is to put prayer in the right order. God first. I make contact with him. I express thanksgiving, praise. He's the object of worship. I sense his fellowship.

After a time of praise I start talking about my concerns. That's the place to speak of needs. Sometimes the sense of my guilt overwhelms me and I confess before I pray for others. Or Ralph's need for a job and Evelyn's troubled marriage weigh heavily on my mind. Guidance for a decision I'll have to make this afternoon. Guidance so that I'll not be led astray by evil. This becomes the improvisation on the true prayer. And only an honest disciple can pray this prayer earnestly.

As I look at the entire Lord's Prayer two main teachings appear. Two basic concepts. First, God's overall interest in humanity. His supremacy in life. But his caring, too. His caring as a father cares about his children.

The second concept is that the totality of life— needs, guidance, forgiveness, whatever—are also concerns for us to take to him.

This prayer summarizes all true prayer. It's a balanced prayer. In seed form, it covers earthly and spiritual needs.

Once we've grasped these basics, we pray with freedom. Not just copying the lines Jesus set forth. God is meeting with us. Right now. We talk to him with intimacy. We share everything with him.

That's a form of real happiness—being in fellowship with the Father who created us and loves us.

*For if you forgive others the wrongs they have
done you, your Father in heaven will forgive you.
But if you do not forgive others, then your Father
in heaven will not forgive the wrongs you have
done.*

MATTHEW 6:14-15 TEV

I'LL FORGIVE YOU IF...
A forgiving spirit!

That's certainly one of the basic characteristics of the
Christian life. We grow by learning to put the past
behind us. That means putting our pains, hurts,
bruises and slights into the box of forgetfulness, seal-
ing it tight and throwing it into the garbage can.

The Apostle Paul wrote, "One thing I do, forgetting
what lies behind and straining forward to what lies
ahead . . ." (PHILIPPIANS 3:13 RSV). Joseph, betrayed by
his brothers and sold into slavery, later became a powerful man in Egypt. He embraced his brothers, blessed
them and forgave their crimes against him (GENESIS
45:15). Jesus taught Peter the law of forgiveness—"Forgive someone up to 490 times"—a figure of speech
indicating continual forgiveness. He called out the
words of forgiveness from the cross, "Father, forgive
them." (LUKE 23:34). Stephen, the first martyr of the
church, cried out, "Lord, do not hold this sin against
them (ACTS 7:60 RSV).

None of these examples, however, speaks of forgiving when another person asks for it. Forgiveness is

based on grace—undeserved, unearned forgiveness. We forgive each other *in response* to our Father's forgiving love. We have experienced God's love and know what it's like to have our sins pardoned.

A fellow minister told me of the death of a parishioner. "I stayed with the father until the hour he died. He refused to forgive his son who had disobeyed him and left home thirty years earlier. He even left instructions that the son wasn't to come to the funeral. That man died unforgiving . . . and unforgiven." My friend had linked the two together—unforgiving on the part of the dying father; yet unforgiven himself. The two go together.

The Apostle Paul puts it this way: ". . . forgiving one another, as God in Christ forgave you" (EPHESIANS 4:32, RSV). ". . . forgiving each another; as the Lord has forgiven you, so you also must forgive" (COLOSSIANS 3:13, RSV).

God forgives unconditionally. That's His nature. Because of the loving and free sacrifice of Jesus Christ, we are forgiven. God places no conditions on our forgiveness. We simply accept it.

Our attitude toward people shows how much we perceive of God's forgiving us. If we cannot and do not forgive, we haven't really experienced absolution from sins. To be freed is a momentous experience. After we experience God's wiping the pages clean, his love within us enables us to forgive those who have wronged us.

That helped me grasp Jesus' meaning in the Lord's prayer. Our forgiving is in direct proportion to our forgiving others. Taking the New Testament as a whole, we realize that Jesus' words don't make our forgiveness contingent upon our forgiving another. But if we refuse to forgive, the evidence points out that we have not experienced true cleansing ourselves.

The words stuck in my throat that Sunday morning. I couldn't finish. As on many other Sunday mornings I monotoned through the Lord's Prayer. Today I couldn't say, "Even as we forgive. . . ." My summer assistant was leading the prayer. I was glad. That meant probably no one noticed my silence.

Milton's face appeared.

Forgive Milton? Why, I'd forgiven—*No you haven't, Cec. You say you have. But there's still anger stored up inside. Every time his name comes up in conversation—even after not having seen him for six years.*

That inner voice had it right. I was willing to forgive anytime he admitted his failures. When he confessed all that he had done wrong to me.

"Forgive us . . . even as we forgive. . . ." *Lord, I was innocent. Milton lied about me!*

". . . even as we forgive. . . ." *The things he said about me. Africans wrote back and told me. Then when Roy came home on furlough I heard even more. And—*

"Forgive us . . . even as we forgive. . . ." *Father, that's not fair! I've always been willing to forgive Milton . . . if . . . if . . . if only he'd ask for it. You can't base your forgiveness on whether I've settled things with Milton.*

"Even as we forgive. . . ." *Or could you base your forgiveness on our forgiving?*

The story about Milton was an old one. It had gone on for years. He had humiliated me in front of other missionaries as well as Africans. He had put me down. And to make it even worse, he was insensitive to the way he treated me. He did the same to other missionaries. A cutting reply. A gentle, but snide remark. A raised eyebrow. I prayed for Milton—daily and fervently. But I don't suppose I ever really forgave him! Mostly I prayed, "Convict him, God. I'm willing to forget it all. Just make Milton repent."

That Sunday morning when the words stuck in my throat, I thought about Milton again. Was an old, unsettled matter keeping me out of fellowship with God? Later in the day I whipped out my Greek New Testament. I felt I could find a way out of that verse. After all, God didn't base his forgiveness on our forgiving someone else! Surely not!

I read Matthew 6:14-15 several times. It didn't help to check out the Greek. Translations didn't give me any escape. Neither did commentaries. No matter where I read, the answer remained the same: Unless we forgive people who sin against us, we remain unpardoned.

Caught. The struggle began again. I prayed, asking God to forgive me. Of course, it wasn't settled even then. Perhaps I enjoyed nurturing that bitterness. After all, he had wronged me! For several days I prayed about the matter. It took me that long to pray and to mean it.

"Lord, I forgive Milton. I forgive every attack against me—whether real or imaginary. I forgive him."

I felt a deep peace inside. That settled my struggle with Milton and with forgiveness. I've learned that not only must we forgive, it's dangerous *not* to forgive.

Milton had wronged me. He wronged others. One of them was Lee. Over the months bitterness took hold of Lee. He spoke out against Milton, fighting him in every possible way. He used innuendos, exaggeration and, in at least one instance, lies. Lee turned into a bitter, disillusioned man. Our mission board asked him to return home. He had been hurt—but he hurt himself. He refused to forgive. His unwillingness turned to bitterness and that finally destroyed him.

That's what happens when we don't forgive. We

warp ourselves. Evil in other people appears so large. We begin looking for their shortcomings. Suspicions grow. As those suspicions increase, we find ourselves blinded. We don't want to see anything good in the other person. Sometimes we even convince ourselves that the other could never say a kind word or work under any but ulterior motives. Then we're really in trouble.

Alice stopped attending church nearly ten years ago. The pastor had offended her. She has never been back there—or to any other church. I asked her once, "Did you ever confront him and tell him he had hurt you?"

Hah! He knows. I think he did it deliberately. If he doesn't realize how much he's hurt me, then obviously he's a man totally insensitive to people anyway. I'll never go back to that church."

"But, Alice, can't you forgive him?"

"I'll forgive him all right. I'll forgive him if he apologizes to me. He owes me that. Just as soon as he says 'I'm sorry' I'll quickly forgive and stand behind him."

Alice may have to wait another ten years! Or an eternity!

She's missed so much in her church—the fellowship, the opportunity of growing with other Christians. And we do miss so much. Our minds fill up with ugly, evil thoughts. We fantasize all sorts of hateful ideas. When I'm out of sorts with a person, I can't think of him or her with pleasant and loving thoughts.

In fact, I visualize conversations in which I tell him or her off. Or argue—always gaining the upper hand. Or other people find out how right I was in not liking that person. And in those situations, no one comes out a winner!

It's possible to forgive. Jesus forgave. He helps us do the same. As we understand just how sinful we are, that helps. None of us deserves God's cleansing. But he does it anyway. If God forgives, can't we also forgive?

The first real lesson I recall about forgiveness came through Mr. Meisner who owned a drugstore. As a child I loved to read. We had so little money, books seldom appeared in our house, other than those I borrowed from the library. For a long time I visited Mr. Meisner's drugstore, sat down on the floor near the magazine section and read.

One day a clerk yelled, "If you're not going to buy, please leave the magazines alone. You kids soil the pages."

After that I walked into the store, casually made my way to the magazines and began reading rapidly until a clerk told me to leave.

But one day, no one seemed to be watching. And, scarcely without realizing what I had done, I stole a comic book. Easy. I slipped it inside my coat. A few days later I took two of them. A week later another two.

My criminal activities came to an abrupt halt one wintry afternoon. Old Mr. Meisner walked up to the door as I started out. "Son, you have something of mine under your coat."

I didn't look at his face—I couldn't. I unbuttoned my coat and took out the comic books. "I'm sorry, Mr. Meisner. Honest."

"Come this way."

He led me into a back room, made me sit on a hard-backed chair while he sternly lectured me about stealing.

Before he finished I sat there crying. "I won't do it again—honest, not ever."

As we walked back through the store, I saw several pairs of eyes focus on me. He must have sensed it, too. He put his arm around my shoulder and we walked toward the front door together. As he opened the door, he leaned down and said quietly, "I think you've learned your lesson. Anyone who wants to read that badly . . . well, you just sit down and read everything on the racks. Just be careful with them."

"Oh, I will, Mr. Meisner. I will. I promise."

I never forgot old Mr. Meisner. Perhaps that's one reason I've learned about forgiving. *I experienced it.* Not only from Mr. Meisner. But in my relationship with God. People along the way in my life have also forgiven me.

A few times I've struggled over forgiving other people. Like Milton. But in the end, I've made it. It's such a good feeling to know that our failures and sins are wiped away. I like to be able to pray to God to forgive "even as" . . . or . . . because we forgive. . . . It works both ways. We can't be right with God without being right with people. We can't be really in harmony with people unless we make our peace with God.

Forgiveness.

"And forgive us our debts . . . as we forgive our debtors. . . ."

Thanks, God . . . that lesson helps me know I'm growing. That I'm moving closer in my relationship to you. I'm still learning what it's really like to be a Christian.

7

Be careful not to perform your religious duties in
public so that people will see what you do. If you
do these things publicly you will not have any
reward from your Father in heaven. And when
you fast, do not put on a sad look like the
show-offs do. They go around with a hungry look
so that everybody will be sure to see that they are
fasting. Remember this! They have already been
paid in full. When you go without food, wash
your face and comb your hair, so that others
cannot know that you are fasting—only your
Father, who is unseen, will know. And your
Father, who sees what you do in private, will
reward you.

MATTHEW 6:1, 16-18 TEV

PHYSICAL SPIRITUALITY

"I hope my breath doesn't bother you," Charles said,
interrupting our lengthy discussion on the New Testament. "I'm fasting, you know. The first three or four
days the breath smells foul."

"Oh? I hadn't noticed your breath," I replied.

He looked slightly dejected. I wonder if Charles
hadn't missed the purpose of fasting. He didn't need to
share the information with me. Had he honestly been
conscious of bad breath, he could have tried menthol
crystals or a breath spray!

One of the significant things Jesus said about fasting: don't advertise. Keep it a secret between you and
the Lord.

I'm no expert on fasting. During my entire Christian experience I've fasted less than five times (and I don't mean skipping an occasional meal). All of them for short periods—two or three days. But each instance came about because of an inner need in my own life.

Like the first time. Ted mentioned Alice in a conversation. Someone remarked, after telling a humorous incident about her, "How does anyone figure Alice out?"

And I jumped in. "I figure that she's one of the most superficial Christians I've ever known." I answered truthfully, even though no one asked me.

And not to leave it at that, I quickly related two instances to bolster my viewpoint.

I didn't know that Alice's best friend stood only a few feet behind us. The friend walked over and said, "And *I* think you're one of the most judgmental Christians I've ever met!"

"Just being honest!" I quipped.

"Then, I'm just being frank!" She gave me a full smile and walked away.

Somehow I stayed through the rest of the party with my friends. But that night I didn't sleep well. Too late to correct the situation. Impossible to retract my words. I *had* been judgmental. Cruel. I called myself a lot of other names. I prayed most of the night. The next morning I had no appetite. I spent several hours that day in prayer. Food held no appeal.

"Lord, I'm too frank . . . I don't want to be dishonest, but I want to be more loving. Make me more understanding. . . ."

On the second evening peace finally came. Assurance of forgiveness. But more. A realization that God had heard me and would help me. In the future He would help me guard my words. For me and for that occasion, fasting was appropriate.

51

The Bible records several instances of fasting. The individual cases didn't happen because someone decided people "ought" to repent. True fasting *erupts* when the soul knows its worthlessness and its need for a renewed relationship with God.

God commanded the Jews to fast only once annually. On the Day of Atonement, as part of the ceremony of national penitence, they refrained from food for one entire day. Several times the prophets called upon the people to fast as a sign of their genuine repentance (see NEHEMIAH 9:1; JOEL 2;12).

Fasting signifies penitence. When people sincerely repent of their sins, they leave food and the comforts of life and turn to God. King David, a godly man in most respects, perpetrated a series of crimes. He lusted after another man's wife, committed adultery with Bathsheba, arranged for the murder of her husband Uriah, then married the pregnant widow. The prophet Nathan confronted the king. David wept, fasted and expressed deep contrition for his sin (see II SAMUEL 11-12).

Fasting expresses sorrow. The religious leaders opposed Jesus. "You're a great teacher, but look at your disciples. They're not fasting—they're actually enjoying life. Stop them! Make them fast! Becoming a disciple means forsaking everything in the world, and regularly denying ourselves food."

Jesus replied, "My disciples are lighthearted. And why not? They rejoice like guests at a wedding. What need is there for mourning?" Yet even in the midst of the joyfulness Jesus added, "There will be a time when my disciples will mourn. When I'm no longer with them. Time enough for that. Now they rejoice" (see MARK 2:18-20).

Today we hear little about fasting. Perhaps it's time

52

to rethink the matter. The Jews understood the closeness between a person's body and spirit. The two are really one unit. In our modern world, we grasp this more significantly. We now acknowledge that when the mind sickens, the body suffers. Both function (or malfunction!) together. We label it *psychosomatic* illness (*psyche:* mind; *soma:* body). The biblical writers were miles ahead of us. When fasting, they left physical nourishment for spiritual reasons. They didn't refrain in order to bargain with God. Or to demand his blessing. An overpowering sense of guilt or failure hit them, and they fasted. Not by dates on the calendar but by the depth of the situation.

I've known of people who, through their fasting, tried to push God into bestowing blessings. One man even wrote a book about it. He depicted himself as sixty pounds overweight, and a disillusioned minister of the gospel. One day, while reading of Jesus' fasting forty days in the wilderness it struck him. "That's the answer!" He shut himself away for six weeks, occasionally sipping only water. He vividly described his desire for food, the temptation to quit, gnawing hunger pains and phsyical exhaustion. But he persevered. At the end of the forty days he had lost weight and gained a new perspective in life. He told of the great results of his preaching after this experience. His book concludes with this idea: Fasting worked for me. If you want power in your Christian living, *fast*!

Unfortunately, God doesn't always work according to a program. The Pharisees became masters at fasting. Some may have found renewed power through abstinence. I suspect others sought only a gimmick. Or a shortcut to spiritual blessing. I'm not opposed to fasting; it can be valuable. But it, too, can be practiced for the wrong reasons.

Fasting can be a genuine appeal to God. Jonah proclaimed the doom of Nineveh, prophesying destruction. What happened? The people prayed. They fasted (see JONAH 3:5-7). Merely hearing the pronouncement of doom upon the people had that effect. The king himself decreed the day as one of fasting. And God spared the city!

In one of the worst flood seasons in Kenya, in the early 1960's, a group of African Christians began fasting, as an appeal for God to stop the torrential rains. The rains stopped the second day!

Some have tried to "use" fasting. The religious leaders of Jesus' day formalized prayer. They did the same with giving. And with fasting. By fasting Mondays and Thursdays, they proclaimed their obviously superior spiritual status. Why those days? They just "happened" to be the main market days when many villagers came to Jerusalem. The ostentacious fasters had a bigger audience.

And just to make certain . . . they walked through the streets with disheveled hair and soiled clothes. Some went so far as to deliberately whiten their faces to accentuate their pallor. Not all religious people acted that way. Jesus rebuked those who did.

But fasting certainly has its place in the Christian life as an act of self-discipline. It's so easy to become self-indulgent, so one man I know fasts one day every week. "For two reasons," he said. "First, I'm a voracious eater. I'd even chew on the refrigerator if I could digest it! That one day a week helps me bring my appetite under control. Funny, but it helps me all week to keep in mind the need to bring every part of my life under Christ's Lordship."

Then he explained the second reason. "I visited Asia two years ago. I compared my corpulence with emaciated, swollen stomachs. It made me ashamed of myself. Now we donate one seventh of our food bill to world hunger. It may not do a lot, but it does something. I feel better. I believe some starving people are grateful!"

Gay and Fred abstain from two meals a week. Fred said, "We also give to world hunger with the money we figure we don't spend. That's one big reason. Actually, though, I have another reason almost as strong. It's teaching me to do without things. I grew up in a home where we had to have the newest and the best all the time. My folks owned the largest house in the area. A new Lincoln every year. I can remember my mother crying because a neighbor's pool measured two feet longer than ours!"

I'd heard Fred talk about that before. He had felt encumbered by the bonds of affluence. "Someone said that a real test of your life is to list the number of things you can live without. Fasting is one of the ways by which I've learned to re-evaluate my whole life. Most of us not only eat too much but too much of the wrong kinds of food. Our self-imposed fasting has helped Gay and me continue rethinking our values."

Gay added, "Actually, missing meals helps me appreciate the good things! I always feel gnawing pains when I miss a meal. That makes me appreciate food when I do eat! Fred and I are learning to enjoy everything in life so much more."

Jesus condemns the wrong kind of fasting. But He doesn't eliminate fasting from the Christian life. He tells us how not to fast when we do.

Perhaps fasting could be a significant experience in our society which is so rich and well-fed. Maybe all of us ought to try it!

*Don't save treasures on earth where rust and
worms destroy, and thieves break in and steal.
Instead, save treasures for yourself in heaven,
where rust and worms cannot destroy, and thieves
don't break in and steal. For your heart will
always be where your riches are.*

MATTHEW 6:19, 20 TEV

TRAPPED BY TREASURES

Sam's eyes misted a little as he talked to me that cold
November. "Yes . . . I grew up with Bill Bickell. He was
my best friend right through high school." I listened as
he retraced incidents of the past—little anecdotes,
snatches of conversation. "The thing that stands out
most vividly in my mind is our senior year of high
school. A revival preacher came to town that spring
and stayed nearly three weeks. Bill and I both got
converted.

"But from there on our paths went different directions. I went on to college, feeling I could best serve
God by preparing to teach. I've been teaching now
nearly a quarter of a century and don't regret it at all.
Not Bill. He saw things differently. One day he said,
'I'm going to make money—lots of money. Then I can
do more for God's work.' I remember so well that
statement."

I knew the rest of the story. Bill made money—becoming one of the wealthiest men in that Chicago
suburb. He remained a member of the largest church

in town, served on the board of aldermen, directly owned or controlled a share in several of the major enterprises. He developed several apartment complexes. Everything Bill touched turned into profit.

Sam and I attended Bill's funeral together. We walked past the open casket for a final view of the body. Afterwards Sam remarked, "It's such a shame, isn't it? He left a lot of wealthy heirs behind. I wonder what he ever did for Jesus Christ." I wondered, too. Bill got trapped. Trapped by treasure. In the beginning he meant well. Earn money to do more for the work of Jesus Christ. But as the dollars rolled in, he lost that initial vision. Life went out of focus. He forgot why he was accumulating the wealth.

Lives easily get out of focus for any of us. And wealth can be one of the surest causes. Jesus warned, "It is easier for a camel to go through the eye of a needle than for a rich man to enter into the kingdom of God" (MATTHEW 19:24). Faith coupled with obedience opens the doors of heaven, not money.

Zacchaeus had gotten his capital by dishonest tax collecting. When he met Jesus, he volunteered to refund what he had stolen (LUKE 19:1-10).

A rich young ruler came to Jesus asking what he had to do to gain eternal life. Jesus said, "Sell what you have and give to the poor." Why this answer? Joseph of Arimathea, a man of wealth and influence, donated his tomb for the burial of Jesus. Cornelius did great acts of charity for the Jews. Neither man is told to sell all his possessions. They both apparently knew how to handle their money. They could be wealthy but didn't let their treasures enslave them. Rich Abraham is called a friend of God (GENESIS 12:3). Joseph advised Pharaoh to store grain for future use (GENESIS 41:25-36). Proverbs depicts ants as an example because they preserve summer food to care for themselves in the winter (PROVERBS 6:6, 30:5).

The difference lies in the value placed on the riches. The young ruler put money at the top of his list of priorities. He couldn't become a pauper for the kingdom of God.

Charles owns a drug store 35 miles north of Chicago. In the twenty years I've known him, this man has made money in vast amounts. One time he invented a shampoo-rinse combination which could be manufactured for a fraction of the cost of the name brands and did the work better. One of the large firms in the country paid him more than a million dollars for the patent to keep it off the market. Charles has money. Yet I've seldom met anyone more generous and open to supporting the work of God. For Charles, riches aren't a snare.

Jesus said, "Do not lay up for yourselves treasures on earth . . . where they perish . . . but lay up for yourselves treasures in heaven . . . where your treasure is, there will be your heart also."

The danger is not in having the wealth but in our *attitude* about wealth.

Our Lord warns about worldly goods. If we expand time, energies, abilities on making money and accumulating possessions, we might well succeed. But when we leave this earth, what do we have?

Jesus spoke the Sermon on the Mount to a group of poor, illiterate Galileans. They sat listening to him on a hillside—fishermen, farmers, tax collectors. His first twelve followers numbered among the poor of the land. Yet he warned them of the danger of wealth.

Treasure—having it or grasping for it—involves risks and can eventually result in total loss. Wealth in Jesus' day was partly in fabrics—rugs, hangings, clothes. Vermin threatened the stored treasures. Thieves could break through the mud or plaster walls of Palestinian homes or dig up the buried possessions. Tools rusted.

Today Jesus might speak of inflations, depressions and the uncertainties of the economy, but his warning would still be the same: "You can't take it with you."

After my military discharge I went to college. We had to struggle to barely exist. Each day when we prayed, "Give us this day our daily bread," we meant literally, "give us *this day*" . . . a hand-to-mouth existence.

Now my life style has changed. I don't have great wealth, although I'm comfortable. I know we have food for this day . . . and tomorrow . . . as a matter of fact we have plenty until Shirley goes to the supermarket again on Friday. Day-to-day existence no longer troubles me.

But worldly accumulations still trouble me.

I find all around me the constant temptation to grasp more. To hoard. To accumulate. To let possessions possess me.

Edna and George taught me more about the use of possessions than anyone else I've ever known. They had seven children. George had no professional training and no great talent. Very average people. Their attitude made them different.

From that family with a moderate income went out money and clothes to everyone in need. People constantly shared with them and they in turn passed it on to others.

Once Edna said to me when we were going through an especially hard financial trial, "We used to pray to God to provide our daily needs. We don't pray that way anymore. Now we pray, "Father, provide for us and a little more so that we can help provide for other people.' And you know what? Money, food, and clothes pour in. I feel like a forwarding agency around here!" Her infectious grin accentuated the joy that she and George had discovered in their sharing.

"Well, I'm safe," Mary comments. "Hank and I don't have any real money. We're struggling barely to pay for our home and educate our children."

"Are you safe? Perhaps your home is your treasure. I know, Mary, the meticulous care you give it, the hours you spend polishing silver and dusting. I'm reminded of how you spent days selecting each single item of furniture for every room. Maybe your wealth is in your bone china and monogrammed silver."

"Shouldn't our house look nice?" she asked me.

"It depends on what the house means to you. Does cooking food or cleaning house come before God? Is the house where you derive satisfaction and pleasure? Your beautifully furnished and gorgeously landscaped home may be the treasure of your life."

Treasures come in many forms and sizes. It may be a husband . . . a child . . . a style of life. I read in the newpaper that a man paid nearly $100,000 for a 1933 Dusenburg car. He said he never planned to drive it. Reportedly, he paid the money so he could sit inside the car and admire it. I'm not trying to judge the man and his motives. I do bring into question what happens to us when accumulation becomes our focus in life.

Real happiness doesn't revolve around having or not having. It revolves around the right view in life. The Bible calls us pilgrims . . . strangers in this world. That's another way of saying we're only here a short time. The value of our lives is not in what we leave behind or what we accumulate while we're here. It lies in what we make of ourselves while we're living.

60

Hebrews 11, often called the faith chapter, lists all the great heroes in the Old Testament. Their commitment to God counted. They stood firmly in their trust. They're the ones God honored, even though they were sometimes despised by the people of the world.

Riches don't last forever. Even if they endure, we don't. When we concentrate on possessions, in the end disappointment imprisons us.

A few years ago one of the wealthiest and most talented actors committed suicide. A star of motion pictures for more than three decades, the winner of an academy award, married and divorced from two of the famous Gabor beauties. George Sanders killed himself. He left a note saying that life was a bore. Even among the famous there's no guarantee of happiness.

Real happiness is concentrating on the right kind of treasure. And Jesus said, "Where your treasure is, there your heart will be." Lord, where is my heart?

The eyes are like a lamp for the body. If your eyes are clear, your whole body will be full of light; but if your eyes are bad, your body will be in darkness. So if the light in you turns out to be darkness, how terribly dark it will be!

No one can be a slave to two masters; he will hate one and love the other; he will be loyal to one and despise the other. You cannot serve both God and money.

MATTHEW 6:22-24 TEV

GOD *AND*...

"There *is* nothing else," the famous actor said.

"But what do you do between roles? How do you live?" the talk show host asked.

An actress sitting to the right of the host replied, "There is no living in between. You're always getting ready for the next part. You wait for a phone call from your agent. Or you read scripts. Or you look for possibilities yourself. But in between, you exist. You don't really live."

Another guest on the television program, a psychiatrist, explained that people who commit themselves to their vocations—any vocations—get what they strive for. For those people, their jobs become their entire world. But they pay a price. "You get out of life what you work for. And you pay 100 percent of the retail price for everything you get."

No one gets everything out of life. Yet we try. We want all the world has to offer and then heaven as a double bonus at the end. Life doesn't operate quite like that! Just being alive forces us to make choices. For Christians, it means we have already made one significant choice. We've put Jesus in the center of our existence.

I still have a lot of problems there—even after more than twenty years of dedication to Jesus Christ. I still like being my own boss, running life as I see fit, making decisions which seem wise to me. That doesn't mean wanting to eliminate God's help. I want Him involved!

And what Christian doesn't want God to have part of his or her life? During periods of depression, we find comfort in his presence, guidance in making a significant decision, assurance of divine protection in danger. But much of the time we like to decide our own course of action. It's almost like asking, "Hey, God, going my way?" We're not trying to leave God out. We simply don't want him only. God's in the picture. Not the total center, but in the picture. It's God *and*. . . .

I graduated from seminary at the top of my class. That same year, by carrying a full load in a university, I also received a master's degree in education. I had a direction. I wanted to teach in a seminary. A good idea. A logical choice. By background and training, teaching had been a large part of my past. Experience teaching in the public school, then in a parochial school. One year's teaching in a Bible college. It was the natural path for me to take.

Add two more ingredients: First, being at the top of the seminary graduating class won me a scholarship. Then, I discovered that I had nearly a year of educational benefits still available under the G.I. Bill. A perfect set up. And out of a dozen applications, in a program where only three students where chosen, I was one of them. This may sound simple and easy. Prayer played a great role all along. I sought God's guidance. I prayed for the doors to open. Everything went smoothly. Then I had a miserable year of school and dropped out!

Now I think I understand some of it a lot better. I wanted to teach and I wanted to teach Bible or religious subjects. God's work was my goal, but I realize now that my desires, my prayers, my movements were always God *and*. . .

"Lord, show me your will," I prayed hundreds of times. Did I really want his will? Or did I honestly mean, "God, you do want me to earn my Ph.D. and then teach in a seminary, don't you? Lord, I want *you* . . . and . . . I want my own will." And that's where the trouble comes in. True discipleship reminds us that a conjunction never follows *God*. It's never God *and*. It's always God, period.

Jesus, in teaching this concept, used the human eye. He spoke of the eye (the singular used for both eyes) in a figurative way. That eye isn't the source of light for our body but it is the guide on which our body depends for direction and illumination. Because of the eye, we're able to make use of the light. This single organ becomes the body's light.

But that light needs a single focus. No diverting. No sidetracking.

If the eye is diseased, the body fills itself with darkness and doesn't function properly. It blurs, or sees double images.

Or take a lamp, for example. Beams shining in one direction illuminate the object. But diffused light weakens the visual image. Singleheartedness. That's the message of Jesus Christ. And we arrive at singleheartedness by choosing it. Choices seem so varied. Endless. But ultimately the choice narrows to an alternative—God or mammon. Not a hundred possible masters, but two.

Jesus taught about the choice always before us. Sheep or goats. Figs or thistles. Wise virgins or foolish. Right or wrong. God or the world. The broad road or the narrow. The alternative has many names. It's always God *or*. There is really no such choice as God *and*. To say "and" already speaks of a choice.

Jesus said, "No one can serve two masters." One master gets an undue share of concern. The other reaps neglect or is ignored. I like to translate Jesus' words, "No one can be a slave to two owners."

Slave and owner. A relationship first-century Christians well understood. In one sense, slaves weren't people but objects. They held no rights and became the exclusive possessions of their owners. No property rights. No time to call their own. For the twenty-four hours of each day slaves belonged to someone else. A slave would never ask, "What would I like to do? The question was, "What does my master wish?"

In several letters, the Apostle Paul introduces himself as "Paul, the slave of Jesus Christ." Those words testified of a submissive relationship to Jesus Christ. Perhaps that's where we have our problems. We like singing, "What a friend we have in Jesus." The words of "Amazing Grace" thrill us and "In the Garden" puts many into a contemplative mood. But what about "Have Thine Own Way, Lord"? That makes us uncomfortable. Perhaps we like to sing the way I saw a hymn listed in a church bulletin: "Take My Life and Let It Be." That may well express where many of us are. We want God's hand upon us—but we also want him to "let it be"—let us alone!

Take my hands and let them move
  At the impulse of Thy love.
Take my feet, and let them be
  Swift and beautiful for Thee...
Take my will, and make it Thine;
  It shall be no longer mine.
Take my heart, it is Thine own;
  It shall be Thy royal throne...

Jesus said we can't be loyal to two masters at the same time. He can't be part of a compound subject in a sentence. Not God and wealth. Not God and fame. Not God and influence. Serving God may be the hard way. The lonely path. The thankless job. But it's also the path of happiness. And true happiness comes when life's goal is singular.

My first commitment as a Christian is to live in subjection to Jesus Christ. And he promises to do me good. To make me a better person. More loving. More kindly. Perhaps it boils down to the age-old problem of rebellion. It started in the garden of Eden. It has continued throughout all history.

When my daughter Cecile was three, I took her into a large department store with me. She kept wanting to go down a particular aisle. "No, honey, there's nothing down there you want to see." That didn't satisfy her. She kept insisting. Finally I said, "All right. Go look." She took three or four steps down the aisle, looked briefly at a shelf and came back. She probably couldn't have articulated her action. I felt sure she wanted to go down that aisle because I didn't want her to. That's the way we start in life. And we're always caught in that temptation.

That explains a lot of the tension and troubles in life. Trying to serve two gods. Two masters. Two ideals. It never works. Jesus' statement about two masters really rephrases the Old Testament commandment, "Thou shalt have no other gods before me." The command-ment not only hammers out, "no other gods alongside me," it means *no other gods*. If God comes first, he comes only!

That's what makes life happy. A unified focus. Con-centrated. Or that word we like to use so much in church: committed.

On vacation one summer we heard a seminary stu-dent preach his first sermon outside the classroom. He had a good message—he had seven or eight good messages! He threw out a little about righteous living, a little about the moral issues of war, a few thoughts on women's liberation, and concluded with a call to repen-tance. His message hit like buckshot. He struck in all directions, concentrating on nothing. He never suc-ceeded in communicating anything specific. "He tried to reach everyone in the congregation," my wife com-mented, "and I'm afraid ended up missing everyone."

To succeed in any endeavor of life means to commit yourself to that activity. The professional athlete, the success-oriented business executive, the successful novelist, all have one secret in common: they work toward a specific goal. They pursue that goal with total concentration.

Like Bill. He bought a defunct electronics firm. In less than three years, the business instead of losing money netted well over $30,000. Why? Bill told me himself.

"I lived for my business twenty-four hours a day. I read everything I could, talked to people, looked at the business plans and programs of competing companies. I made friends for the sole purpose of furthering my business. Everything I did for more than two and half years was calculated for the end result of making my business successful."

Bill made it. He paid the cost: he sold himself out.

That's really the theme of Jesus' teaching: selling ourselves out for God. That's another step toward true Christianity!

10

This is why I tell you: do not be worried about the food and drink you need to stay alive, or about clothes for your body. After all, isn't life worth more than food? And isn't the body worth more than clothes? Look at the birds flying around: they do not plant seeds, gather a harvest, and put it in barns; your Father in heaven takes care of them! Aren't you worth much more than birds? Which one of you can live a few more years by worrying about it?

And why worry about clothes? Look how the wild flowers grow: they do not work or make clothes for themselves. But I tell you that not even Solomon, as rich as he was, had clothes as beautiful as one of these flowers. It is God who clothes the wild grass—grass that is here today, gone tomorrow, burned up in the oven. Won't he be all the more sure to clothe you? How little faith you have! So do not start worrying: "Where will my food come from? or my drink? or my clothes?" (These are the things the heathen are always concerned about.) Your Father in heaven knows that you need all these things. Instead, be concerned above everything else with his Kingdom and with what he requires, and he will provide you with all these other things. So do not worry about tomorrow; it will have enough worries of its own. There is no need to add to the troubles each day brings.

MATTHEW 6:25-34 TEV

WHY PRAY WHEN YOU CAN WORRY?

God cares about you. Do you believe that? Do you believe that God loves, not just the world in general, but you in particular? That you're special to God?

I used to think that was a silly question. Of course God loves me! I've always been taught that. Lately, however, I've realized how many people need convincing of God's love. They know he's love or that "God so loved the world that he gave. . . ." "I know God loves Harold or Philip or Margaret or preachers and missionaries, but I can't believe he loves me." Perhaps statements like that come from people partially because they don't love themselves.

Last year George, an ordained minister, resigned from the parish. After two traumatic years and the breakup of his marriage, this man really suffered. But he's through the worst part of it now. Only recently he said, "Now I know how much God loves me. I used to think that if I worked harder, or built up a bigger church, God would like me more. Even though I said it often enough, I never realized that God is *Father* and I'm a son—not a slave. He loves me. Now I know that!"

God cares. That's the simple message Jesus taught. And because God cares, worrying is groundless. Even dishonoring. Feverish anxiety says we don't trust God to stick with us in the hard places!

The Hebrews left Egypt's cities and reached the Red Sea. Until that point they had taken everything calmly. God provided the means of escape. They were freed from their captors. Then they saw the Egyptian armies coming at them. And in front of them was the Red Sea. No escape. They grumbled. God had let them down. The Lord of heaven had to separate the sea before the people realized his protection was still upon them.

Later, in the wilderness, they encountered problems

of hunger, thirst, and attacks from the Amalekites. Each time they grumbled. "Has God brought us out into this desert only to leave us? Will he let us die out here and let people say he couldn't bring us into the land?" They never learned their lesson! The God who loves is the God who cares. The God who cares also provides for his people.

Jesus said, "Don't be anxious." When we translate that phrase into English, it sounds weak. "Don't be distracted by cares. Don't let worry get the best of you." Perhaps that gets a little closer to Jesus' meaning. He wasn't saying not to think ahead. And he taught that we need to count the cost before embarking on any venture. But he referred to the kind of concerns or situations that take our minds away from God. As he said in the parable of the sower, "The cares of the world . . . choke the word" (MARK 4:19).

Four times in these verses Jesus tells us not to worry (see verses 25, 27, 31, 34). The message isn't against exercising sensible concern about life, but is against worrying about what we can't help anyway. Foolish anxiety only harms ourselves. It really does us no good.

Jesus gives several examples. Birds take no care. They work, spending time in making nests and acquiring food. But the birds also stop to sing their song! Flowers bloom, wither and die. It's all part of the cycle of nature. Worrying doesn't help us grow taller or, as the verse probably means, does not help us add any time to our lives. In fact if we worry enough we may be able to shorten it!

In Jesus' day poor people heard his teaching. They understood and took his words literally. Not to worry about food for each day. Not to be concerned over clothes to wear. Many of his hearers lived an almost

71

hand-to-mouth existence. His words must have brought great comfort to them.

In our affluent world, we may have different kinds of concerns. But the lessons still apply, whether our worries center on "Where's my next meal coming from?" or "How can I make the mortgage payment, pay on the three charge accounts, and still give an offering to the church this month?"

In the past few years we've learned that the economy can change overnight. The fuel crisis. The financial crunch. Blizzard conditions in the south that even brought snow to Miami and snow flurries to the Bahamas. Crop failures. Constant articles questioning the soundness of the Social Security funds.

What's secure today? Who's really able to say, "I'll never have to worry about daily needs?"

Jesus' words have a startling relevancy for us. "I gave you life, won't I take care of that life? Stop worrying. I'm around." That's the word of comfort to God's people. We don't need to worry! Worry says we don't trust.

During my early days as a pastor, Minnie made this lesson clear to me. "I just don't know what I'm going to do. Everytime you turn around the cost of living goes up or some new taxes are put into effect!" Minnie angrily thrust the newspaper at me.

"See that!" She pointed to an article about the proposed new stadium. "They'll start building it next year. You know what that means?" Before I could respond she answered her own question. "Taxes go up! They say in the article that admissions will pay for the cost but you know how these politicians are. They promise it will cost nothing and you end up paying through the nose.

"Then look at people like me. Our income is fixed, and taxes go up. I'll have to move from my apartment.

Or give up the telephone, or cut out something. I barely make it now." Minnie went on calculating the impending hardships she would suffer because of the proposed stadium.

"Minnie, have you prayed about it?"

"Prayed?" For a moment she looked at me as she seemed to think seriously. Then a smile formed on her cheeks. "No. I suppose I'd rather worry!"

Aren't many of us like that? It's easier to worry about troubles, problems, and what might come to pass than to attack them head-on. And why not? To worry takes little effort. We just let ourselves go, allowing our minds and our wills to have free reign. Without restraint, we can soon worry about everything from radiation fall-out to the price of imported plastic goods.

To worry pays well, too. Ask any doctor or druggist. You reap untold migrane headaches, ulcers, heart attacks. You easily influence others. Announce your current worry; before long half the people you know worry alongside you.

Years ago while I was a member of a midwestern church, the pastor preached on honoring the Sabbath. "Sunday is a God-appointed day of rest and worship. Rest from our labors and toils and a day to worship God and enjoy the fellowship of the house of God." He hit hard on the topic. John owned a chain of statewide independent supermarkets. His stores had been staying open on Sunday. At the conclusion of the service, two people noticed that John left the sanctuary "quite angry and upset."

When he heard about the incident, one of the deacons said to another, "John's the best single giver in our congregation. If he gets angry and leaves . . . it'll throw our budget for sure." The deacon who heard that remark passed it on to a friend, adding, "If John fails

73

to keep his pledge, we don't know what the church will do. We'll probably have to cut down on foreign missions or one of our programs."

Within two days, most of the members of the congregation knew and fretted over John's action. They hated to see him leave the church. Not only the principal source of income, he also taught Sunday School and could be depended upon to serve on any committee when asked. For the rest of the week the people worried, talked back and forth, and feared for the existence of their church.

On Sunday John returned to service as usual. One bold soul asked, "John, you looked upset last Sunday when you left. Anything wrong?"

"The pastor was right—I knew it all along. At first I got mad, thinking he had no right to tell me how to conduct my business. After I got home I realized he hadn't told me. He had only given me the Word of God. At the end of the month I'm closing my stores on Sunday. I'll lose money but for me this is the right thing to do."

Isn't worry really useless? Jesus said, "Don't be nervous and anxious about food, clothing. God takes care of the earth, he'll take care of you. Your worry won't help. The most it can do is make you frantic and hasty in your decisions. Trust God."

I think Peter understood that message. In Acts the Apostle is arrested and put in prison. James had already been killed, Peter awaits his sentence. A miracle occurs.

> And, behold, an angel of the Lord appeared and a
> light shone in the cell; and he struck Peter on the
> side and woke him, saying, "Get up quickly."
> (ACTS 12:7)

74

How anxious, distraught, nervous is the Apostle? So disturbed the angel strikes him on the side to awaken him! Here lay a man not knowing if death were around the next corner—sleeping!

Jesus makes it clear that anxiety over the future proves futile in the long run. To care is right; to prepare is common sense; to worry is a mockery of religion. Jesus not only gives the negative injunction, "Don't be anxious or overly concerned." He also points in the positive direction.

His answer: set up priorities. Put God first. If he's first, everything else falls into its proper place.

I recall that one of my professors used to say, "If you make God's business your business, he'll make your business his business."

That's a modern twist to Jesus' words: seek first his kingdom and his righteousness, and all these things shall be yours as well.

What things? The things specifically mentioned in the preceeding verse. He promises clothing, food, the basics of life. God knows our needs. He's giving assurance that if His kingdom holds first place, our needs will be met.

We have the choice. We can fret. Let worry consume us. Nervous anxiety eat away at us. Or we can pray. And trust. Trusting adds that sparkle of happiness in the Christian life. No need to worry: God's around. And he cares.

11

*Do not judge others, so that God will not judge
you—because God will judge you in the same way
you judge others and he will apply to you the same
rules you apply to others. Why, then, do you look
at the speck in your brother's eye, and pay no
attention to the log in your own eye? How dare
you say to your brother, "Please let me take that
speck out of your eye," when you have a log in
your own eye? You imposter! Take the log out of
your own eye first, and then you will be able to see
and take the speck out of your brother's eye.*

MATTHEW 7:1-5 TEV

I SEEN THE BAD YOU DONE

Henry's shrill voice rang out, "I seen the bad you done!"
With those words he ran toward the kitchen door.
"Mommy! Mommy! Come, see the bad Ralph done!"

Mother hurried out. On the grass sat Ralph, staring
at the scene in front of him. He had cut an earthworm
in half.

"Him's bad. Mean. I telled him so!" shrieked four-
year-old Henry.

Ralph, two years older, looked up as though suddenly aware of what had been happening. "I didn't do
anything bad."

"You did! You did! You kilt the worm. You cut him in
pieces."

"I didn't hurt him. See, both halves can move. Naw, I
just felt sorry for the poor worm. He crawled along the

76

ground all alone. He felt lonely. I wanted to give the worm someone to play with."

Henry had judged and passed sentence on his older brother. He observed an action, pronounced Ralph guilty of wrongdoing. "I seen the bad you done."

Unfortunately many people, unlike Henry, will continue talking like that the rest of their lives. They'll learn to say it more grammatically. Perhaps even with more cultured tones. But the intent will remain the same.

Most of us judge other people's actions. When we censor another's action we never think of ourselves as malicious, evil, disobedient to God's commands. Yet we do exactly the opposite of Jesus' expressed word.

"Judge not!" taught the Lord.

The words mean, "Don't be censorious in your judgments." Or "Don't be critical of people."

When Jesus says, "judge not" his words should be taken in the sense of judging and condemning. In life we constantly make judgments. We could not function as useful human beings if we didn't. Jesus called Herod a "fox" (LUKE 13:32) and the Pharisees he called "hypocrites" (MATTHEW 23:14). A few verses later in Matthew we are told not to give holy things to dogs. We must make some kind of determination of who falls into the category of "dogs." When in Matthew 7:15 we're told to be wary of false prophets—how can we, unless we consider and categorize?

"Judge not" means, "Don't condemn people by their actions alone." When we see a situation, or hear words, our tendency is to catalog it in terms of good or evil, right or wrong. We pounce upon an action and in our adult vocabulary echo Henry's words, "I seen the bad you done." "Don't pass sentence on another person," Jesus says.

First, we don't know all the facts. Henry knew only the act committed by Ralph. He never inquired about the rationale. The act of cutting the worm in half may have been wrong, but Ralph was motivated by compassion. His error was factual, not ethical.

A church in our community prepares hot meals five days a week, then distributes them to needy people at little or no charge. One recipient lived in a practically-new house, costing somewhere in the neighborhood of $60,000. After the first visit, one of the distributors called the pastor. "I believe in helping the poor and the hungry. But I don't have a house anywhere nearly as nice as that one. If that woman can live in that mansion, she can buy her own food!"

The pastor explained. "She owns the house. Her husband died recently and she's lost everything but the house. It's paid for. But she has nothing else. She lives on welfare and has no one to help her."

"Pastor, if I had only known. . . ."

How many times have we had to utter those words? If I'd only known the true facts, all the facts, the whole story.

In seminary we evaluated the sermons of other members of our class. This evaluation included not only the sermon material but the delivery and style. After Jim had preached I said, "You have a very difficult voice to listen to. It's extremely nasal. At times I strained to hear certain tones. You really ought to work at improving it."

Tom turned to me and said sharply, "Don't you know Jim was born with a cleft palate? He has had several operations to repair it. You think he's bad now—you should have heard him three years ago."

If only I had known! He had no marks of a hairlip. The plastic surgery had been skillfully done.

Second. We can't pass sentence on another because

78

we're not fit to judge. Only God judges rightly. Our own prejudices and opinions blind us. An adulterer condemns the homosexual; the alcoholic sneers at the gambler. "I may have an awful temper but I'm certainly no thief." Haven't we all heard "I may be a . . . but I'm certainly no. . . ."? Comparisons and judgments—always putting ourselves on top, always failing to realize we're blinded by our own failures and limitations.

When I pastored a church in a newly transitional area, three black children began attending. During morning worship they got up several times to get a drink or use the rest room. Afterwards I heard stormy words about the disturbance of those children. One elderly brother smiled and said, "Odd, isn't it? For years our own children have run back and forth to the drinking fountain during the service. Never heard any complaints about them!"

There's an even stronger reason against judging with a censorious spirit: The standards we use to judge others by also become the standards used to judge us!

> *For with the judgment you pronounce you*
> *will be judged, and the measure you give will be*
> *the measure you get* (MATTHEW 7:2).

This works in two ways: First, people judge us by the standards we set. If we constantly criticize and belittle others—and especially in their absence—how will people respond to us? In the same way. When the name Madeline comes to my mind, I think of a malicious-tongued woman. Or Hank symbolizes for me raw gossip. Those people have earned their identification. They know how to measure the spirituality of everyone inside or outside the church. But most people guard their tongues around those two!

Some years ago one of the best-known preachers in

79

the Southwest left his wife and three children. He had been carrying on an affair with a married woman who, in turn, left her husband and three preschoolers. It caused quite a scandal that people discussed for weeks. Why? Was that preacher the first man to commit adultery and abandon his family? Or course not. And it wasn't because of his fame.

The man represented moral standards. When he degraded himself, his holy calling and the church he served, people felt appalled. Some harsh judging took place. Because he had been in an esteemed position and fell, some people felt elevated by maligning him.

Second, God judges us according to our understanding. If I know the wrongness of lying, it becomes a much more serious sin for me when I lie than it does for a person who has never heard the law of God.

Mary Slessor, a pioneer missionary to Calabar, West Africa, in the nineteenth century, encountered Africans who murdered twin babies. Murder is always wrong. But to them and in their culture, killing the infants meant chasing away evil spirits. Could we believe that God's punishment of an African following his own culture could be as severe as a murderer in our Western culture?

Jesus taught this very principle in a parable in Luke 12:42-48 and concludes with these words:

> *But he who did not know, and did what deserved a beating, shall receive a light beating. Everyone to whom much is given, of him will much be required; and of him to whom men commit much they will demand more* (LUKE 12:48 RSV).

In the Old Testament, a Persian named Haman hated Jews. He worked zealously for their destruction.

80

Part of his plan included building a scaffold for the execution of Mordecai, the Jewish leader. God overthrew his plan: Haman himself hanged on the noose he had prepared for an enemy. As we judge, we shall be judged.

Some years ago we made a few table rules in our home. One was that we take as much as we liked of anything but must eat what we took. A second rule: we must at least eat a little of everything. We have steadfastly enforced this rule since our children were small. Once I tried to sneak away from the table. I had left several bits of radish on my plate. Hoping not to call attention to that fact, I picked up my own plate to carry it to the kitchen.

Wanda, my eldest, called out, "Hey, Daddy, you've got to eat that! You know the rule."

"But honey, I just can't stand radishes. Besides, this is hot."

"That's not fair. *You* made the rule. Now you want to break it for yourself but you make us kids eat everything."

I ate each bite. Once we set the standards by which we judge life, be careful. We have then set up the very standards by which God will judge our actions and deeds! Now we understand more easily why Jesus cautions us.

The positive side is: straighten up yourselves first. Get number one in order. Once we are walking in the right way, we can see a little more carefully about judging others. Oddly enough, the people I personally consider to be the holy ones—the real saints—are not the judgers! I wonder if you've noticed this.

In fact, one of the godliest men I've ever known in my life walked down the street with me one day. A drunk staggered past us, nearly knocking me down. I gave him a disgusted look. My friend said, almost in a mumble and certainly not as rebuke to me, "But by the grace of God . . . there go I."

Perhaps that's one of the true marks of happy Christians. They love without judging, accept without condemning. They never say, "I seen the bad you done."

12

*Do not give what is holy to dogs—they will turn
and attack you; do not throw your pearls in front
of pigs—they will only trample them underfoot.*

MATTHEW 7:6 TEV

THE RIGHT WORD AT THE RIGHT TIME

Jesus didn't treat everyone alike!

He didn't even give them all the same message. He treated Peter with patience, like a teacher with a slow learner (JOHN 21:15-19). Yet he denounced the scribes and Pharisees, the very ones who should have been the most perceptive. Jesus pronounced a curse upon Capernaum which had failed to respond to his teachings (MATTHEW 11:3), but he wept over Jerusalem (LUKE 13:34).

Earlier in Matthew 7 Jesus warned his disciples against censorious attitudes. He urged, "Don't condemn or prejudicially judge." Here he balances his statement. "Don't be indiscriminate. Be careful to whom you speak and what you say."

The message of God's love may be beautifully effective. People may be converted through it. But the same words may make another curse.

Two hundred years ago Jonathan Edwards preached his most famous (although not his greatest) sermon called "Sinners in the Hands of an Angry God." In that message he graphically described the terrors of hell and eternal punishment. People upon hearing the sermon cried out in repentance. It is said that some grabbed the pews in terror.

In the mid-1950's a prominent evangelist preached that same sermon, using the same words as Jonathan Edwards. It produced a quite different effect. No people gripped the pews. No one screamed out for mercy.

Edwards preached an appropriate message to an appropriately prepared people. The evangelist apparently didn't have the right word for the right time.

"Don't give holy things to dogs" is another way of saying it. To the Jews, a dog was a scavenger, not a housepet. To call a man a dog heaped upon him the lowest form of contempt. Abner, in quarreling with King Saul's son, says, "Am I a dog's head?" Another way of translating that for contemporary readers might be, "Could I do such a lowdown thing?" Jews sometimes used the term "dog" in referring to non-Jews—showing great contempt for those outside their own race. In Jesus' day large, savage dogs roamed almost everywhere, prowling through garbage and rubbish. Old Testament writers refer to them in the most derogatory way (see PROVERBS 26:11, PSALM 59:6, ISAIAH 56:11).

One of the signs of God's special curse was to be eaten by dogs. After Queen Jezebel had Naboth killed so that her husband could confiscate his vineyard, the prophet Elijah opposed the wicked monarch.

> *"And concerning Jezebel, the Lord says that dogs will eat her body in the city of Jezreel. Any of your relatives who die in the city will be eaten by dogs, and any who die in the open country will be eaten by vultures"* (I KINGS 21:23-24 TEV).

A few years later Jehu rose to power. He raced toward the palace to overthrow the wicked queen. Palace officials threw Jezebel out a window. Later Jehu ordered her buried but scavenger dogs had already eaten her body (II KINGS 9:30-37).

Another term, equally as despicable, was "swine." The dietary code of Israel forbade the tending of pigs or the eating of their meat. When someone called you a swine or a pig, you received the greatest insult possible.

This is probably because God listed swine among unclean animals which were not for consumption (LEVITICUS 11:7, DEUTERONOMY 14:8). In fact according to Isaiah (65:4; 66:3, 17) eating pork was an abomination.

Imagine how godly Jews must have reacted when Jesus told his parable of the prodigal son. To show the extent of the young man's degradation, he says,

> *So he went to work for one of the citizens of that country, who sent him out to his farm to take care of the pigs. He wished he could fill himself with the bean pods the pigs ate, but no one gave him anything to eat* (LUKE 15:15-16 TEV).

Jesus said that the pigs, if fed pearls, would trample on them. Not satisfied, they'd even attack those who threw the inedible to them.

We don't know exactly what Jesus meant about pearls or holy things. We do know that pearls were fabulously priced. They came from either the Persian Gulf or the Indian ocean. In a later illustration Jesus said that a merchant would be willing to sell everything just to possess such a pearl (MATTHEW 13:46).

Someone has suggested that pearls resemble peas or acorns in size. If fed to pigs, they would greedily taste a few. Quickly discovering they were inedible they would angrily attack the tricksters, Jesus suggests.

I believe Jesus meant us to discriminate in our witnessing to God's love. Giving the wrong message to the wrong person at the wrong time in the wrong place is comparable to giving holy things to scavengers or precious jewels to pigs. Let's be careful that we don't purposely cause people to scorn. How frequently have we noticed the way the Protestant preacher is portrayed on TV and in books? He's a fanatic who screams, "Repent! Mend your ways!" He becomes an example of the ridiculous.

God has given us the Bible, but not everyone responds to truth. Some will receive at one time and on other occasions be quite closed.

Val attended our church for nearly a year. A pleasant young woman, but she simply showed no evidence of responding to the gospel. Then she visited out of town and went to church with relatives for three Sundays. When she came back, she said, "Oh, Mr. Murphey, I realize now how much I need Jesus Christ." Imagine my surprise! She told of the church she had visited. "You've always preached about how much God love me and forgives me. I guess I never thought of myself as being a sinner. But when I heard that preacher, it really made me think. I've sinned so many times. Now I realize how bad I was!" That other minister spoke to Val at the right time and with the right kind of message!

In the life of the Apostle Paul we read evidence of that right timing with the right message. When he spoke to King Agrippa, the monarch trembled. On another occasion while imprisoned, Paul along with Silas sang hymns and praised God. An earthquake struck and the guard fell down, crying out, "Sirs, what must I do to be saved?"

In still another situation, Paul preached in Antioch of Pisidia. Many listened. Jews attempted to prevent his preaching. Finally after much struggle Paul said to the Jews, "It was necessary that the word of God should be spoken first to you. Since you . . . judge yourselves unworthy of eternal life, behold, we turn to the Gentiles" (ACTS 13:46).

A few chapters later, and following Jewish opposition, the Apostle declares, "Your blood be upon your heads. . . . From now on I will go to the Gentiles" (ACTS 18:6). He left them. This staying or leaving often presents a dilemma. Paul seemed to move on when people no longer responded. Yet, a century ago Henry Martyn went to Persia and preached for many years. No converts professing faith in Jesus Christ. Why didn't he "cast the dust from his feet" and go to a new city or a new country? Why does one person persist in a place year after year, and have little to show in terms of results? Another moves from place to place, staying only short periods in each location, and yet sees great results. Are those who stay doing so out of stubbornness or the will of God?

Bud and Fay Sickler labored in the "bush country" of Kenya from 1945 to 1953. They achieved a limited amount of success. In 1953 they moved to the coastal city of Mombasa. They worked with almost no success for four years. Then, in 1957, a revival spirit hit. Through their efforts, many churches sprang up in the coastal region. The Sicklers left the upcountry area; other missionaries stayed. Who was right? When does one move on? When does one doggedly stay in a place regardless of the lack of results? That's where the leading of the Holy Spirit is so important. He is the one who leads us to speak the appropriate words at the needed moment. Or leads us to retreat into silence. Or to stay and labor on. Or to move to a new place.

At a stage in my life when I searched and longed for the truth of the Gospel, I attended a crusade in Chicago. I didn't understand the sermon for it was filled with theological jargon. As I went out the door, a zealous young man grabbed my arm. "Are you saved, brother?" I had no idea what he meant. I didn't even answer. "You can be, you know. Right now. Just give your heart to Jesus." I mumbled something and hurried from the auditorium. I thought he was some kind of fanatic. No one had ever talked like that to me before.

Weeks later I attended a service for the first time in a different city. Being in the military service, I wore my uniform. A middle-aged woman came up to me. "I don't think I've ever seen you here before. Are you from the Navy base?"

"Yes, I am."

"Would you like to come home for dinner with my husband and me? We often invite servicemen when they attend our church."

For the next two hours I was in their company. They said little about God; they showed much. Their courtesy and kindness spoke so much to me.

As I left, I thanked them as profusely as I could. I had been lonely that day and they had made my day pass quickly.

"We're so glad you could share this food with us. We—we don't know how to talk about God very much, but we try to show people we care. Anytime you visit our church, I want you to know you're welcome for dinner with us."

"Thanks—thanks a lot!" I appreciated her sincerity and honesty.

If I were paraphrasing one of Jesus' parables I could say, "Which of the two showed the message of God's love? The young man or the middle-aged couple?" The right words at the right time! That's why we have the Holy Spirit in our lives. That's also what makes us happy Christians. As we mature, we learn to rely more and more upon him to guide our witness for Jesus Christ.

13

Ask, and you will receive; seek, and you will find;
knock and the door will be opened to you. For
everyone who asks will receive, and he who seeks
will find, and the door will be opened to him who
knocks. Would any one of you who are fathers
give his son a stone, when he asks you for bread?
Or would you give him a snake, when he asks you
for fish? As bad as you are, you know how to give
good things to your children. How much more,
then, your Father in heaven will give good things
to those who ask him!

MATTHEW 7:7-11 TEV

YOU CAN'T MAKE IT ALONE

"I had to talk to you about the message you preached last Sunday," Adelle said as she called me aside. "I needed to hear a sermon like that. You see, I've always been so hesitant about praying for myself and for my own needs."

"I think a lot of us need that reminder," I replied.

"I've always been told by teachers and preachers— or at least that's what I think they've said—to pray for other people all the time. I've always felt so—so guilty when asking God to help me."

She paused for a moment, looking at my face, to make certain I understood. I nodded. "When—when I ask for myself, something makes me hesitate. Then I usually say, 'God, I hate to ask you this, but . . .' Your sermon last Sunday helped. This past week has been so good for me. Now I feel free to talk to God about myself as well."

This incident illustrates Jesus' words in Matthew 7:7-11. We are to ask God. And part of asking God is to ask for ourselves. Some older commentators make quite a case for growing intensity. They say it like this: asking shows some desire; seeking indicates a greater desire; knocking signifies the utmost intensity.

When asking, we imply consciousness of a need. We also signify that an inferior is appealing to a superior.

Seeking incorporates humility but goes beyond. It implies action. An earnest petitioning, yet more. The Bereans heard Paul teach about Jesus Christ. But they were different from the people to whom the Apostles had preached at Thessalonica, where Paul and Silas were run out of town. "Now these Jews were more noble than those in Thessalonica, for they received the word with all eagerness, examining the scriptures daily to see if these things were so (ACTS 17:11).

Knocking is asking plus seeking and persevering. When I visit friends and know they're home, I knock. Or I ring the bell if they have one. If no answer, after a few seconds I knock again. I'll keep on knocking until they open the door.

Using three verbs which all point toward a single idea, Jesus shows the importance God places upon our asking him to help us in our times of need. And giving the exhortation in triplicate is God's way of stressing the matter.

This same statement appears in the Gospel of Luke. There the triple exhortation concerns God's teaching on prayer. The disciples found Jesus praying and said, "Lord, teach us to pray like John the Baptist taught his followers." He gives them "The Lord's Prayer," followed by the three-fold exhortation. Luke's setting is different, but the purpose is the same as Matthew's. Luke's message says, "You want to pray? Okay, then, ask . . . seek . . . knock. In Matthew, the command to pray follows strong negative statements: "Don't judge . . . Don't give holy things to dogs. . . ." Then, almost as if the Lord anticipates our admission of failure, He says, "I understand. You can't do it alone. Now you have the privilege of asking for help. If you really want help, tell me about it."

These verses not only tell us that we *may* ask, but actually *command* us to! Ask and Jesus assures us that we'll receive! When we tell him our needs, he doesn't turn away. As a matter of fact, since God commands us to ask, isn't *not* asking a sin?

Jesus said, "Ask . . . seek . . . knock." If we refuse to petition God, aren't we disobeying?

People hesitate. "Who am I to ask for the Lord to intervene in my life?" "There are so many other people in the world who need him more than I do." "My problems seem so petty compared to those of a lot of people I know."

Jesus still says, "Ask . . . seek . . . knock."

I remember when I was about ten and my younger brother Mel was eight. We had gone downtown with my dad in his old 1937 Ford. Dad went into Sears to buy spark plugs for his car. While he was taking care of that, Mel and I explored the rest of the store. At that age, anyone could have predicted where we stopped: at the candy section. We didn't have a penny between us, yet we looked. We saw coconut candies, chocolates, jelly beans, circus peanuts, mints, peanuts, maple clusters. Naturally we wanted them all. Mel and I whispered back and forth.

"If I had a dime," I said. . . . Then I considered seriously whether I would buy circus peanuts or jelly beans or a maple cluster. Nope, not the maple cluster.

You only got one of them for a dime. For ten cents I could get a lot of jelly beans.

Mel quietly walked around the entire candy case, poking the glass with his fingers. He even backtracked and stared a long time at the caramels. "Circus peanuts," he whispered. "I'd spend the whole dime on them."

"Well, I changed my mind. I think I'd like those cinnamon drops. They're hot but they're good. And if we got them, then we wouldn't have to share so many with everyone else 'cuz everyone doesn't like them."

Mel stayed firm on his decision. I changed my mind several times. But all along we knew we had no money.

Then we saw Dad coming. I wanted to ask him to buy candy for us, but I felt it wouldn't do any good. He had been ill a long time and had only recently returned to work. I hung back, staring for the last time at the candy, wanting to fill my mouth with chocolates. But I said nothing.

"Hey, Dad, can we have a dime?" Mel asked. "We want some candy. They've got circus peanuts here."

Without a word, my father reached into his pocket, and handed Mel a dime. We had candy that day.

Mel asked. He wanted the candy. Unhesitatingly he appealed to our father.

I didn't expect to get any money. And, being a little more shy, I wouldn't have considered asking. If it hadn't been for my younger brother, we wouldn't have gotten candy either.

This illustrates prayer for me. It's realizing we can't handle everything by ourselves. We call on the God who won't let us down. Remember the parable of the prodigal son? He couldn't make it by himself. He tried. He left home. But when he had exhausted his own resources, accepting his own failure, he returned to his father. And the father was waiting for the son. He saw him coming. He never asked, "Have you repented? Have you come to your senses?"

The father hugged his son, prepared a feast, and provided new clothes. And he said to everyone, "This is my son—the one who was lost—now he's back." That's how our Father treats us. Always waiting and always caring.

We come to God out of our sense of need. "Father, I can't handle it by myself. I need you." To admit, "God, I can't do it," doesn't mean we're weak. It's really a declaration of faith. When we say, "I can't" we're also saying, "God, you can!"

When my son was six years old he became aware of his physical prowess. One day I started carrying groceries from the car to the house.

"Daddy, let me carry the biggest one!"

"Here, son, take this bottle of bleach. It's lighter."

"Please, Daddy, the biggest bag. I can carry it. I know I can."

After several minutes of his pleading, I finally said, "Okay, John Mark, you try. Now I'll hand the bag to you. If you find it's too heavy, will you tell me?"

He nodded with the kind of nod that said, "Of course this bag isn't too heavy."

I took two other grocery bags and headed toward the house. Before I got inside the house, I heard a voice crying out, "Daddy! Help! I'm dropping it!"

He struggled to hold the heavy load. He had gone less than ten feet from the car. Tears swelled up in his eyes. I quickly laid down my load and ran toward him. "Hey, son, it's okay. You tried. One day you'll be stronger and you can carry it by yourself."

I took the heavy bag in my right arm, and grabbed my son with my left and we went toward the house.

"Daddy, you're strong, aren't you," he said.

My son had tried. It was okay that he couldn't do it alone. But his father could.

One of my favorite poems by Annie Johnson Flint says:

> His grace has no limits, His love has no measure.
> His power has no boundaries known unto men.
> For out of his infinite riches in Jesus,
> He giveth and giveth and giveth again.

The more we recognize that we can't stand alone, the more we have to ask for his help. And that's what God wants—for us to recognize our dependence on him. We don't have to be afraid to ask. God's always willing to give to his people.

Every Sunday morning I give a children's sermon in my church. On one Sunday after the children had come to the front, I held out a doubled fist. "I have a nickel in my hand. How many of you believe I have a coin in my hand?"

All the children raised their hands or vocalized their belief.

"Do you really believe I have a coin in my hand?"

"Oh, yes," they cried out.

"Now, if you really believe I'm not lying to you, then one of you will come up here and take it. It's in my clenched fist."

There was a great deal of giggling and whispering. Finally one boy stood up and cautiously walked toward me. The rest watched closely.

The boy opened my fist and there was a nickel in it. He smiled, took the nickel and started to sit down.

One little boy said, "I was going to get up and get it."

I wonder if that isn't the way a lot of us are. "I was going to do it." Hesitant to ask. Unsure of God's willingness to answer prayer. But we don't need to wonder. Jesus keeps saying, "Come! Ask. Receive. It's yours." I can ask! What wonderful freedom that gives me. Being a Christian, and being one who realizes his need for help, encourages me to ask. I'm no longer the shy ten-year-old, afraid to ask because he expects to be turned down. Now I'm the growing Christian. I know he's my loving Father because I've experienced his love. He urges me to turn to him for help. He reminds us that when I exhaust my resources, his help is just beginning.

Do for other people what you want them to do for you: this is the meaning of the Law of Moses and the teaching of the prophets.

MATTHEW 7:12 TEV

LOVE...BUT WHOM?

Charlie wore a tee-shirt with these words boldly printed on it:

> *DO UNTO OTHERS...*
> *BEFORE THEY DO IT UNTO YOU*

He bought it as a joke. A clever take-off on the Golden Rule. Yet, it is a philosophy of life. There are some who attempt to live by such a life style. "Get the other guy before he gets you."

What a sad existence. A world of killing off competition, getting the advantage over your competitor. You work to outthink, outmaneuver, outsell. You have to beat him to the punch—getting the most at the beginning.

And what do you get out of it all? An ulcer? A heart condition? Perhaps a fat bank account? But what a lonely life, too!

The level by which most people live, I suspect is this:

DO UNTO OTHERS AS THEY DO UNTO YOU

If my neighbor is friendly, I respond in kind. If I get

a cantankerous, snippish one, I treat him the same way. That's never God's way. Jesus said, "If you greet your friends and ignore others, you're no better off than a heathen. Why, even the unbelievers do that much."

But most of us live that way: kindness to kindly people; ugly thoughts toward ugly-acting people. Such a position may be justifiable—but no Christian ought to be satisfied with this kind of existence.

A friend and I bought some groceries together on a single ticket because he had no cash with him. When we got to his house, we checked out the sales slip so that we could settle the account. We discovered the clerk had missed ringing up three cartons of coke, on his part of the bill.

"Aren't you going back to straighten it out?" I asked.

"Naw. Don't worry, those supermarkets make up for it plenty. They purposely overcharge some people so they can come out all right for losses and thefts."

We can live that way. All too often, even when we know better as Christians, we still allow life to function on such a low plane.

If you hear that John doesn't like you, how do you treat John? Do you go out of your way to be friendly? Do you attempt to communicate with him? All too often we retort, "Well, if he feels that way, I'll just avoid him."

We know it's immature when a teenager says, "Bad rumors have started at school about me. If that's the way people look at me, I'll be that way—give them something to talk about!" Such an attitude never benefits anyone—you or the other person.

Several times in marital counseling I've heard a wife say, "He started chasing other women. I decided two could play the game as well as one! So when he ran around, so did I." Yes, people *can* and *do* live on a level like this. It's not a happy level, and it's far from the real potential in life. God has so much more ahead for us.

That's the third level of life. It says:

> *DO TO OTHERS EXACTLY*
> *AS YOU WANT THEM TO*
> *DO TO YOU*

This level presents the greatest challenge to Christian living. It does away with petty feelings and differences. We begin to live as Christ wants us to.

But wait a minute! You've heard all that before. What new thing have I pointed out to you? Nothing. We've heard it over and over and over. But have we lived it over and over and over? Has such an attitude been practiced in our lives? How realistic, how practical have we made this principle?

Yesterday morning I drove to my church. The right lane is plainly marked, "RIGHT TURN ONLY." A lot of cars filled both lanes. As I started to drive forward, being properly in the left lane, a Chevrolet pickup truck barged in from the right. I let him go past—after all, his pickup looked bigger than my little car. As he forced his way in, I observed a bumper sticker on his fender: "Christ is the answer." I wondered as I drove along behind him how much of an embarrassment his action must be to the cause of Christ. As I thought further, I realized how often *my driving* denied the principle of treating others as I want them to treat me.

For example, in a spurt of impatience, I honk my horn at the fellow who doesn't take off immediately when the traffic signal changes (but get angry when someone blows at me!). I get furious on the freeways when a slow-moving vehicle insists on controlling the fast, left lane. Yet, sometimes I've been guilty of just that. Once I recall driving at 70, then the top speed limit, in the left lane. A car rapidly approached from the rear, and came right close behind me. I said, "Hmph, 70 miles an hour is fast enough for anyone," and didn't budge. Yet . . . would I have liked to be treated that way?

During my first year in seminary, we moved into seminary-owned apartments. One or two neighbors introduced themselves. Largely, however, no one paid much attention to us. It became rather lonely during those first few weeks. I had come from a different part of the country than the rest, the only Northerner in the Southern school; I had a non-Presbyterian background among all Presbyterians; I was nearly ten years older than most of the students.

I promised myself that things would change the following year. The next summer as new students moved in, we visited them immediately, helped them unload when possible, offered them a meal and gave any assistance we could. We had known what it meant to want friendship and not have it.

Several weeks after Shirley went to work, one secretary began complaining about another employee. Shirley stopped her co-worker immediately. "Ruth's my friend. I don't want you to say anything against her to me." Stunned, the secretary shook her head, "I wish I had a close friend like you!"

Why do friends betray *us*? We may need to ask instead, how do we treat them? Are we dependable regardless of their action? What kind of friend do you want? Be that kind of friend to another.

A quiet, lovely lady in our congregation lost her sister a few weeks ago. Women in our church began calling each other about taking food to her home. One of them said to me, "She was always one of the first people to respond to any need. When she heard of sickness, you just knew she'd be on the doorstep before long."

Is it any wonder the other ladies of the church responded to *her* need?

Do you want to be loved? Love somebody! Want to be liked? Then don't be unkind or belittling to others. The question to ask in doubtful situations is this: "How would I like to be treated?" When we can answer that question, we know the direction to take.

Isn't it wonderful that Jesus gave us such a grand principle? It avoids the necessity for dozens, even thousands, of rules of conduct. "When someone cheats you out of money, then you . . ." Or "If. . . ."

Jesus said the observance of this principle is equal to the Law and the Prophets. That is, this sums up their teachings. While these words are not found specifically in any Old Testament writing, the implication is there. We treat people as we wish to be treated.

Yet, who can do it without God's help? Pride, anger, egotism, fault-finding—all these keep us from putting into practice the highest values in life. We need God's help. More, perhaps, than the pickup truck driver knew, Christ is the answer. But he's not the answer, unless we ask the question! Knowing the question and the answer—internally knowing—that's how we're part of God's family.

15

Go in through the narrow gate, for the gate is wide and the road is easy that leads to hell, and there are many who travel it. The gate is narrow and the way is hard that leads to life, and few people find it.

MATTHEW 7:13-14 TEV

BETWEEN A NARROW PLACE AND A HARD WAY

"Come in through the narrow gate!" That's Jesus' exhortation. His metaphor says more than starting at a constricted entrance; the pathway itself continues to be narrow. These cryptic words tell us the story of discipleship. We come to Jesus through only one door. Only one means of access.

I once saw a religious cartoon filmstrip. People came to Jesus Christ and had to pass a narrow door. Many of them couldn't make it through. One man tried to carry a bag containing many possessions. He could make it through, but his goods could not. An obese woman couldn't make it through. She had put her appetite and desire for all the finer things of this life first. To enter through the narrow gate meant saying "yes" to Jesus and "no" to herself. She walked away dejected and sad. Someone else didn't make it through either. A famous person, he had to have his admiring audience with him. No space for them all. Because the gate was wide enough for only one person, the famous personality backed away. He wouldn't go it alone.

From the first pages of the book of Acts, the disciples realized they had many things in common with their

102

Jewish friends: belief in the Old Testament, acceptance of prayer, almsgiving to the poor. But on one point they disagreed and because of that issue, they could never bridge the gap.

Peter said it like this:

> *Salvation is to be found through him alone; for*
> *there is no one else in all the world, whose name*
> *God has given to men, by whom we can be saved.*
>
> (ACTS 4:12 TEV)

Because of that conviction, coupled with their refusal to stop preaching about Jesus Christ, Peter and John suffered. They were beaten, warned, and later imprisoned. But their choice had been made.

On a later occasion, Luke records:

> *The apostles left the Council, full of joy that God*
> *had considered them worthy to suffer disgrace for*
> *the name of Jesus* (ACTS 5:41 TEV).

Life constantly presents us with choices. It brings us to crossroads at which more decisions have to be made.

And we do make decisions. Even standing still is a choice.

Moses cried out to the people, "See, I have set before you this day life and good, death and evil. If you obey the commandments of the Lord . . . then you shall live and multiply and the Lord your God will bless you . . . but if your heart turns away . . . I declare to you this day, that you shall perish" (DEUTERONOMY 30:15-18 RSV).

Joshua, at the end of a long life, faced the people in a farewell appearance. He declared, "Choose this day whom you will serve . . . but as for me and my house, we will serve the Lord" (JOSHUA 24:15 RSV).

Jeremiah, speaking to the people, in the last days

103

before the Babylonians captured the people and destroyed the land, said, "Thus says the Lord: Behold, I set before you the way of life and the way of death" (JEREMIAH 21:8 RSV).

God constantly confronts human beings with choice, and many of us make that initial and great decision to come to Jesus Christ.

It's the hard road that lies behind the narrow gate which troubles us most. Lance learned what it meant to walk that road.

"Mom! Dad!" he said as he burst into the house after a four-hour drive from college. "I've great news to share!" You've always tried to get me to church and to serve Jesus Christ. I just wasn't having any of it. Then recently, through friends at college, I had a real experience with the Lord!"

Lance's parents showed pleasure and happiness over this news. The young man went on to say, "And now I know what I'm to do with my life. For the first time, I have real guidance and a purpose. After I finish law school next quarter, I've decided to work with Legal Aid here in town. There are so many people who can't properly afford lawyers and legal help. This is my chance to serve Jesus Christ!"

Lance expected a rousing response to his words. Instead, his father quietly asked, "Are you sure, son? Can't you serve Christ in a—a good legal office? I mean, we need Christians in every walk of life."

"Agreed, Dad, but here's the difference: I feel this is God's will for me."

"Lance, darling," replied his mother, "I think you're being a little hasty. Take more time to think about it. You'll see things differently, I'm sure."

Lance left his parents' home a few minutes later. He felt bewildered. Hurt. Even a little angry. Their attitude was hard for him to grasp. For the next several

104

hours he walked the streets, reviewing the conversation in his mind. And not only the conversation of that day—but the hundreds of other days when they had urged him to surrender his life to Jesus Christ.

"They've talked to me for years about God. And now—now that I've turned myself over to him, they're the ones who want to talk me out of doing his will."

He prayed over and over for the Lord's guidance about his future. With or without parental acceptance, he concluded his work was to assist the poor.

"Lance, you're only throwing away your life," his uncle said.

"Such work for you?" queried his aunt. "You're such a brilliant young man, Lance. People who won't do anything to help themselves—well, it's just a waste, that's all!"

His family never understood. He felt the loneliness. The isolation from his own family. Relatives and friends called him a fanatic.

"Sure," he admitted, "some of the people don't appreciate what I'm trying to do. But I'm doing this for God. However, I also get satisfaction from those who do care. The way they thank me over and over. Or the tears of happiness I see, as though I had given them an expensive gift. I don't regret my decision—not in the least!"

Lance never wavered. He had his sense of direction. He often felt the stabbing pain because the people closest to him didn't understand. He learned by experience what it meant to cut himself off from the protection and understanding of his family.

But then Jesus never said life would be easy for a disciple. Following him doesn't automatically merit everyone's respect and admiration. Jesus didn't promise an easy journey. From various places in the Gospels, we know he promised persecution from enemies, even

105

sometimes from our own families. He said people would misunderstand us. Once he said, "If anyone wants to come after me, he has to deny himself, take up his cross daily, and follow me" (LUKE 9:23).

In a seeming wave of emotion, a wealthy young man offered himself to Jesus. "I want to follow you." But Jesus rejected him. The price of discipleship was more than the young man could afford.

Taking our stand of obedience to Christ may not win us popularity polls. Compromise may appease people, but it doesn't honor God.

In 1959, years before the full impact of civil rights hit the South, a pastor in Alabama took his stand. He knew the message wouldn't be received well. He knew there would be serious aftereffects. But he also felt that as a servant of God he had a mission. He concluded his sermon: "In God's eyes, all people are equal. We don't find that only in the Constitution of the United States. The concept permeates the whole of the New Testament. To refuse fellowship to people because of the color of their skin is not Christianity. Negroes are part of the people of God as much as we are. And he holds us accountable for our attitudes and our actions toward them."

Largely because of that sermon he was forced to leave his pulpit. He felt rejected not only by the congregation but by most people in that city. He had ministered in that church almost ten years, building it from a small neighborhood congregation to a church of 1500 members.

Years later, when I met him, he said, "I wouldn't want to go through the pain again—especially to hear the name-calling and bigoted things people said . . . but I'd still do it again!"

In the early centuries of Christianity, believers railed against the brutality of gladiatorial games, calling

106

them barbaric. Today most people agree. But 1600 years ago few people listened.

In the late 1930's and 1940's, some Christians sheltered Jews, saving them from gas chambers or exile. They themselves were killed or imprisoned.

In the 1940's a minority of Christians cried out, "War is wrong. To kill never honors God!" We incarcerated many of them and humiliated others because they attempted to live by their convictions. It was a very unpopular stand—but by the 1960's we were hearing those same words shouted across the country.

What am I saying here? It is not enough to think as others think or to act as others act. To say, "Well, they're good Christians and they do it," doesn't excuse us. Jesus warns that the life dedicated to him is one of hardship. The popular way, he says, leads to destruction.

That's not intended to discourage, but only to dispel illusions. Jesus promises no easy way or simple life. He does promise joy for sorrow, comfort for our mourning, and strength for our difficulties.

The choice always lies before us! We can stay with the crowd, walking closely beside them, saying the things they say, never stirring up controversy so we'll not hurt anyone's feelings. That's the broad way.

The narrow way means faithfulness to Jesus Christ! And faithfulness means following Jesus Christ regardless of how others react.

The missionary organization under which I worked in Africa took a stand on the issue of polygamy. They agreed that one wife to one husband fulfills the biblical concept of marriage. But, they said, if a man came to Christ already having more than one wife, we accept him as a brother in the faith. He is still responsible for all of his wives. We could not undo the past. All of them could join the church and take the Lord's Supper. But

107

if a man, already a church member, took an additional wife, this was a sin. His conduct became a matter of church discipline.

Other churches disagreed. For them no polygamist could join a local congregation. Only his first wife could become a church member. Only she could take communion. The husband could join only if he got rid of the other wives. Several of the other organizations quarreled with our stand. One even withdrew from fellowship with us. In more recent years most of the other churches have modified their position. But for years other missions shunned us.

Times change. New issues flare up. And God's people speak up from their convictions. They may sometimes be wrong, but they take their stand. Not everyone agrees with my position on abortion, the feminist movement, or euthanasia. But I speak up when the issues are raised.

That's another way of acknowledging that I am a Christian: I stand for what I believe in, even though it places me between a rock and a hard place. Even when no one else lines up with me. Or I'm ignored. Or called bigoted. Radical. Even fanatic.

I suppose in his day Jesus heard those terms used a lot, too!

16

Watch out for false prophets; they come to you
looking like sheep on the outside, but they are
really like wild wolves on the inside. You will
know them by the way they act. Thorn bushes do
not bear grapes, and briars do not bear figs. A
healthy tree bears good fruit, while a poor tree
bears bad fruit. A healthy tree cannot bear bad
fruit, and a poor tree cannot bear good fruit. The
tree that does not bear good fruit is cut down and
thrown in the fire. So, then, you will know the
false prophets by the way they act.

MATTHEW 7:15-20 TEV

PROFESSION AND POSSESSION

Every evening she stood out there. Always the same
large shopping bags. Always the tired look on her face.
I was a teenager and worked three evenings a week. I
lived in an area of a Midwestern city where the buses
ran less frequently after 10 P.M. That only meant that
when the bus arrived, it was always crowded.

I looked at the woman: middle-aged, petite, so thin a
gushing wind might hurl her down the street. As I
glanced down at the bulging shopping bags, I felt sorry
for her. I had watched her over a period of weeks
struggle to get on the bus. One thing I had noticed, no
matter how crowded, someone always offered her a

seat. She'd sit down with such a sigh of relief and profusely thank the donor.

Over the months I got to know her rather well. Her name was Inez. One night the bus was late and we talked quite a while. As the bus pulled up, I reached down for her bag. "Here, let me carry it for you."

"Oh, no thanks. I can manage."

"Really, Inez, I don't mind. Here, let me give you a hand."

She smiled brightly and said, "I wouldn't think of letting you. I can manage."

"Seriously, I'd like to help."

"Look, kid," she replied with frost in her voice. "There ain't nothin' in them bags but cotton. I been doin' this fer ten years. Never fails to get me a seat. I go clear to the end of the line. Sure beats standin' all the way."

Inez got her seat again that night. And every other night as long as I kept taking the night bus. People felt sorry for Inez. She looked so frazzled. She professed what she didn't possess.

I've thought about Inez many times over the years. Once in a while I wonder if I'm not like her—oh, in a much smaller way, of course. I wonder if I'm a spiritual failure. I wonder if I don't give the calculated impression of possessing what I'm only professing. As well as I know my own heart, it's not a deliberate deception. But I wonder if I give the impression of being more spiritual, more committed than I really am.

Jesus warned against false prophets. He says they come in the guise of sheep but inwardly are wolves. He implies they approach in meekness and attempt to destroy. They come expressly to mislead. Jesus warned. "Beware of (literally "hold your minds away from") false prophets." They come looking like sheep.

110

Outwardly, nothing distinguishes them. It's what's inside that makes the difference.

The Old Testament speaks often against the false prophet. He doesn't have divine authorization. He brings his own message. Generally, he tells people what they like to hear. During the days of the decline of the Jewish kingdom, Jehoshaphat reigned in Jerusalem and Ahab ruled over the rest of Israel. The two kings arranged an alliance. Ahab asked, "Jehoshaphat, will your armies join with mine as we fight against Ramoth-Gilead?"

The other king said, "Yes, of course. But first, let's call the prophets in. Let them pray and ask God for guidance."

Four hundred prophets appeared. Every voice said the same thing: "Go fight. God will give you victory."

Jehoshaphat must have had some doubts because, even though four hundred men had assured him, he said, "Isn't there another prophet of the Lord of whom we may inquire?"

Ahab admitted, "Oh, there is one. His name is Micaiah. I don't like him. He never prophesies good about me, only evil."

Jehoshaphat prevailed and Micaiah came. His prophecy: "If you go up, you'll be defeated."

One voice speaking against four hundred! Ahab cried out, "Didn't I tell you that he wouldn't prophesy good about me?"

The two armies went out to fight. Jehoshaphat was wounded and died (see I CHRONICLES 18).

False prophets! Ahab believed because they promised what the kings wanted to hear. Not because they proclaimed the truth.

I'm not a false prophet—at least not intentionally. But sometimes . . . just once in a while . . . this passage

111

and others like it disturb me. The Lord makes us focus attention on ourselves. Am I really who I say I am? Do I possess the faith and the dedication that people think I do? Can we conceive of getting apples from peach trees? Or cashews from the pecan? The same principle! God calls me to live and to proclaim a particular style of life—a life that proclaims the good news in Jesus Christ. The sense of failure disturbs me. I suppose that disturbs any true pastor or Sunday school teacher or any sincere Christian.

Do I really possess what I profess? That's quite a question to wrestle with. I saw a poster a few years ago that asked a question like this: If you were on trial for being a Christian, would there be enough evidence to convict you?

Amy Carmichael spent more than fifty years as a missionary in India without a furlough. She gave her entire life to the work. She wrote among other books *God's Missionary.* I read the book shortly after reaching Africa.

The opening chapter tells of a conversation between an Indian woman and Miss Carmichael. The Indian was bitter and angry. She accused missionaries of not possessing what they professed. "And," she said, "you make patterns for us to follow. But you make crooked patterns." Miss Carmichael relates how the words stung her, although she admitted that they were true. Charges like that are thrown at God's people—and, unfortunately, we sometimes deserve them!

A Lutheran pastor and theologian, Dietrich Bonhoeffer, was imprisoned and later executed under the Nazi regime. He wrote a highly introspective poem, "Who Am I?"

He said that prison guards looked at him and they saw him in one light: calm, cheerful, firm. Bonhoeffer bore bad news well. Then he probed deeply into him-

112

self. People see this side, but is that the real Bonhoeffer? He asked if he was really what people said he was. Or was he what he feared and knew of himself. For he thought of himself as restless, sick, struggling, weary, and empty. He was ready to give up.

"Who am I?" That's a question believers should ask themselves. Am I what people see in me? Am I what I perceive about myself that others cannot? None of us is probably as bad as we see ourselves. Nor is any as good. We are probably somewhere in between. I struggle with this a lot. Sometimes they call this the identity question. It hits us in many forms.

I know a lot about myself. I believe, although doubts sometimes plague me. I love Jesus Christ, yet sometimes a selfishness obscures my vision. One day I read my Bible and can hardly believe it when the devotional time ends. The next day it's an effort of the will to read even a single page. At times I point with pride at my accomplishments. Then an inner voice reminds me of other areas that resulted in failure. So I struggle. I'll probably never totally resolve who I am.

Bonhoeffer never really resolved the conflict either. He concludes his poem:

> *Who am I? They mock, these lonely*
> *questions of mine.*
> *Whoever I am, Thou knowest, O God,*
> *I am thine!*

The Apostle Paul must have had the same difficulties, too! He established churches. Pioneered new ground. Underwent persecution and opposition of every kind. The Acts of the Apostles as well as his own letters are filled with the outstanding life and ministry of this man.

But he also seemed to be asking himself, "Is my

profession equal to my possession? After all I've done for Jesus Christ, am I going to fail in the end?" In I Corinthians 9 the Apostle compares the Christian life to competing in a race to win a prize. He concludes, "I harden my body with blows and bring it under complete control, to keep from being rejected myself after having called others to the contest" (I CORINTHIANS 9:27 TEV).

A human being. He, too, wonders about his life matching up to the message he proclaims. I suppose that's common to serious-minded disciples.

In another place Paul, realizing the power of our sinful nature, wrote even more strongly: ". . . when I want to do what is good, what is evil is the only choice I have. My inner being delights in the law of God. But I see a different law at work in my body—a law that fights against the law that my mind approves of. It makes me a prisoner to the law of sin that my mind approves of. It makes me a prisoner to the law of sin which is at work in my body" (ROMANS 7:21-23 TEV).

Bonhoeffer concludes it well for all of us: "Thou knowest, O God, I am thine." With all our failures, with all our shortcomings, we still belong to Jesus Christ. And the Lord loves us the way we are. He exhorts us to possess what we profess. And he'll help us as we work toward that goal!

Lord, as much as I come short of what you ask, I want to serve you. It's that inner desire that convinces me I'm not a false prophet. Like the martyred pastor, Dietrich Bonhoeffer, I, too, can say, "Lord, you know that I am yours."

17

Not everyone who calls me "Lord, Lord," will
enter into the Kingdom of heaven, but only those
who do what my Father in heaven wants them to.
When that Day comes, many will say to me,
"Lord, Lord! In your name we spoke God's
message, by your name we drove out many
demons and performed many miracles!" Then I
will say to them, "I never knew you. Away from
me, you evildoers!"

MATTHEW 7:21-23 TEV

TELL AND SHOW

Chuck always puzzled me. I never seemed to know
what to say to him. For three months he came to our
group. He prayed beautiful prayers. He quoted long
passages from the Bible. His strong baritone voice led
us in singing hymns.

The trouble was, I knew Chuck outside of those
early morning meetings. We worked in the same building. He wasn't hypocritical or covert in his actions. He
blatantly entered into one sexual affair after another
with Waves on the base. Yet each morning he came to
our meeting and prayed with us.

I was a new convert, hardly aware of the Christian
principles of life. But even in my neophyte days, I
knew that immorality was sinful.

One morning as we concluded our worship, Barry
said, "Chuck, how can you act the way you do and still

call yourself a Christian? People talk about you. They says things like, 'Is that the way Christians behave?'"

"What I do is my own business."

Barry shook his head. "Nope, Chuck. First, you're hurting yourself. And you're ruining not only your own testimony, but ours as well."

"Hurting myself? Listen, I'm having fun."

Barry sighed and tried again. "But, Chuck, how can you do things like—like having sex outside of marriage and—"

"Because I believe in Jesus Christ."

He believed. Only the week before in our night Bible study we had talked about faith.

"Faith and only faith makes us Christians. We can't earn salvation. We don't deserve it. It's God's gift. We receive it by believing." That's what the chaplain had said.

The older Christians in our group had nodded agreement.

"Don't try to pull that line on me!" Barry had almost shouted.

"Line? Look, I believe in Jesus Christ. He's my Savior."

"Don't tell me you believe."

"Now you're setting yourself up as my judge?"

"No, Chuck, But I've known you nearly a year. I've never seen any real evidence of your faith. You say you believe. You pray and quote the Bible. But your actions don't match your words."

"You *are* judging. . . ."

"Chuck, don't tell me you believe and then live like an unbeliever. How can you tell me you believe and then commit adultery every week, when Jesus condemns adultery."

Chuck stopped coming. He didn't stop his sexual

activities. We tried to talk to him several times. He gave us the same answer, "I believe in Jesus Christ." So far as I know, Chuck never changed. And in the past 20 years I've met many other Chucks.

Jesus never said, "Just believe." He said, "Not everyone who comes along and says, 'Lord, Lord,' will make it into the kingdom of heaven, only those who obey my commandments."

Paul emphasized salvation by faith. He stated (and perhaps even overstated) his case because he wrote to Jews who tried to earn salvation. They pointed to their morally clean lives, their sacrificial giving, their obedience to laws. Paul tried to say that those qualities, fine as they are, did not produce salvation.

Actually, faith is all we need. But it's more than mental assent. More than intellectual agreement. True faith leads us to right action. Paul says, "The righteous shall live by their faith" (GALATIANS 3:11).

A few years ago I visited a church, and two young girls sat in front of me. The pastor extended an invitation to "those who want to be saved tonight." He said a lot more than that, but that was his appeal.

One girl nudged the other. "Go on up. It's easy."

"I'm scared. I don't know what to say."

The first replied, "All you have to do is say you believe in Jesus. And if he asks you any questions, you're supposed to just keep saying that."

She went forward. So far as I know, her name was then written on the roll of that church. A new member. She *said* she believed. Perhaps she really did. It left some questions in my mind. I'm a pastor. In my concern to help people, I too have been guilty of easing them into the kingdom of God. I don't like people to suffer. I want to help them work past their doubts.

But I wonder if I've not hurt some of those people.

Doubts keep us open to possibilities. Uncertainty keeps us searching.

Recently a woman in our church, in referring to the dogmatic-type teacher of her class, said, "I wish I had the kind of certainty about my faith that he has! He's so—so sure about everything."

"Julie, you may be closer to reality than he is," I replied. "You're honest about your uncertainty. You may be more spiritually healthy than he is!"

"How could an unbeliever know you're a Christian?" a provocative teacher asked her fifth-grade class.

"Because I go to church on Sunday," one boy replied.

"Because I help my daddy pick up church bulletins from the floor and the pews."

The answers varied. In essence they said, "Because I go to church" or "Because of what I do for the church."

Look at my deeds! That's the credentials of many. But is that how the Bible identifies the Christian? Jesus' words in our English translation say, "Not every person who calls me 'Lord, Lord,' will enter into the Kingdom of heaven, but only those who do what my Father in heaven wants them to do."

The words, "not every person who calls me 'Lord, Lord!'" is a Hebraic expression which means "Just talking about your faith isn't enough. Don't *tell* me you believe. *Show* me that I'm Lord."

Samson killed enemies of God's people and yet lived most of his life in disobedience. Balaam prophesied against Barak and the people of Midian. He foretold punishment and destruction. But the prophet never came to be numbered among God's people.

Twelve disciples walked with Jesus nearly three years in Galilee. They saw his mighty works and did some of those deeds themselves.

118

And he called the twelve together and gave them power and authority over all demons and to cure disease, and he sent them out to preach the kingdom of God and to heal. LUKE 9:1-2

Judas stood among that group of twelve. He did the mighty deeds, performed the miracles. He cast out demons. But he never made it into the kingdom of God.

We've all known or heard of the Elmer Gantry type of preacher. The hero of a Sinclair Lewis novel, Gantry preached the gospel of fire and brimstone, quoted the Bible and gave the continual word of the Lord. But between sermons and campaigns the author portrays a weak, sensual man who lived for the passions of the flesh.

We cannot prove our relationship to Jesus Christ by all our good deeds or by the actions we have committed. Calling on his name, doing work in his name establishes nothing. We have too long a line of characters both biblical and nonbiblical who refute that premise.

The question we may need to ask is, "How can I live a Christian life?"

As mentioned earlier, the usual answer is, "I believe Jesus is Lord," "I believe Jesus is God," or "I believe in the Bible." All good answers. But often too glibly stated. Perhaps a better answer might be, "Because I *live* the lordship of Jesus Christ in my life." How do we take the bumps of each day? How much trouble comes our way before we start mumbling, groaning, grumbling, crying? As unpleasantness strikes, can we still believe in the lordship of Jesus Christ? To confess that means that Christ is king, master not only of my life but of all my situations.

119

I remember Brian standing at his wife's side in the hospital. She had been critically injured in a freakish accident. With tears in his eyes, he talked to her. Sally, too sedated to respond, lay silently inert.

"Honey, the doc says you probably won't make it. I don't know how the kids and I'll make it without you, Sal. But God gave you to us and God'll take care of us the rest of the way."

Brian knew the lordship of Jesus Christ!

Is Jesus the Lord in life when a business deal falls through? When we don't get the raise in pay we expected? When our paycheck doesn't quite cover it all? Where's Jesus in our life then?

Another answer people have given me to "How do I know I'm a Christian" is because, they say, "I feel something inside." But they tell me psychedelic drugs do the same thing. The right amount of alcohol or any stimulant can have similar effects. Or symphonic music or the beauty of nature.

As a teenager I read Lloyd Douglas' *The Magnificent Obsession.* Something about that book touched me. It made me want to live as selfless a life as Dr. Hudson had done. But all those feelings and poignant emotions didn't bring me to Jesus Christ.

Someone else answers, "Jesus loves everybody. And I'm somebody."

Right on! But can we presume on that love? He loves. But responding to that love means obedience. It implies commitment to God's will. Being a Christian is not merely thinking, feeling, wanting. Being a Christian proclaims, "I strive to do what God wants!" That's the secret to a true faith. Doing the will of God. It's living a love that responds to God's unmeasurable care.

18

*So then, everyone who hears these words of mine
and obeys them will be like a wise man who built
his house on the rock. The rain poured down, the
rivers flooded over, and the winds blew hard
against that house. But it did not fall, because it
had been built on the rock.*

*But everyone who hears these words of mine
and does not obey them will be like a foolish man
who built his house on the sand. The rain poured
down, the rivers flooded over, the winds blew
hard against that house, and it fell. What a
terrible fall that was!*

MATTHEW 7:24-27 TEV

YOU KNOW I CAN'T HEAR YOU WHEN THE WORLD'S GOT ALL MY ATTENTION

How much do we hear? Sounds flood our ears constantly, but we don't hear most of them. We've learned to screen them out.

I sat at my desk a few minutes ago and decided to listen for a full 60 seconds. I heard the distant sound of car engines because the road is about 400 feet from my study. The low hum of the drinking fountain in the hallway. Far off I detected a siren—perhaps an ambulance. Ordinarily I never notice any of these sounds.

Since we live only ten minutes' driving time from the Atlanta airport, planes fly near us all the time. But we've been here long enough that we block out the sounds. I'm no longer aware of their presence. It's only when we have guests that they notice the noise. Then I'm nearly always startled—yes, planes do make noise. I hear them again, even though they've been coming over our house thousands of times.

We've learned to screen out all kinds of sounds. Unfortunately, we've also screened out God's voice. God's always speaking; we're just not listening. He talks through the Bible, through sermons and lessons. But he also speaks to us through people—their words, challenges, needs.

The sounds pass our ears—we merely let them go by. We do nothing to put into practice what we've heard. The book of James warns us:

> Do not fool yourselves by just listening to his word; instead, put it into practice.
>
> JAMES 1:22 TEV

He goes on to describe the listener who screens out the word of God:

> Whoever listens to the word but does not put it into practice is like a man who looks in a mirror and sees himself as he is. He takes a good look at himself and then goes away and at once forgets what he looks like. But whoever looks closely into the perfect law that sets people free, who keeps on paying attention to it and does not simply listen and then forget it, but puts it into practice—that person will be blessed by God in what he does.
>
> JAMES 1:23-25 TEV

When the Bible speaks about hearing, it means more than words. Hearing God implies the willingness to obey! Jeremiah cried out, "Amend your ways and your doings, and obey the voice of the Lord your God. . . ."

122

(JEREMIAH 26:13). Hearing God's word must be coupled with action. It is not enough to listen. Obedience is needed as well.

Matthew 7:24-27 gives the gist of the Sermon on the Mount. These verses contain the Christian life in summary form. The wise person—the Christian—listens to Jesus Christ. From listening proceeds a dedicated will to live out the received truth. The building of the "house" begins. Day by day work goes on. No expense is spared. That house will withstand all batterings from winds and torrential rains.

The wise builder differs from the foolish in one aspect: the foundation. Apparently both men, in Jesus' parable, built their houses in a valley. During the dry season there was no problem for either—the land is dry and no harm comes to either house.

But the first builder has foresight. He knows the dry season won't last. Soon the sky will darken and storms will beat down. Rains will deluge the building, and winds will batter it. Unless precautionary measures are taken, the house will be washed away by the swirling tide. He thinks ahead. Before constructing the house, he removes the loose gravel, digs down to rock bottom. Then he lays a foundation on the rock. The foolish builder ignores the problem. He builds his house but doesn't dig down to the rock. He erects his house on loose gravel, as though bright days will last forever.

When Jesus explains the parable, he says that "these words of mine" are the foundation. By that he means all the things he says.

Building one's house on rock means not only listening to the Lord, but out of gratitude putting his commands into practice. Hear *and* do what Jesus commands.

The day of testing comes—for both houses. The rain pours down on the houses. It is one of those heavy storms, common to the period of the "latter rain" (about March or April). Cloudbursts. Thunder. Rains seem not to have an end. The lowland fills with water. First a sluggish brook, then a raging torrent. Winds and rain pummel against the buildings. And the house that's built properly stands.

But it takes hardly any effort for the powerful floods to undermine the walls of the other house and carry away the very sand on which it had been erected.

Jesus' parable contains its own application and gives its own exhortation. It's as though he says, "You're sitting here listening to this. Don't just listen. Get stirred up. Get into action."

Of course, action starts with hearing. But the real test of what we've heard takes place when we leave the church or Sunday school class, or close the Bible. What kind of action follows?

One evening I visited prospects for our church. They tried to talk with me, but their eyes kept darting toward the door. Once or twice the wife winced at a banging sound. Finally she said, "Excuse me," and yelled, "Christine! Turn off the television and come in here."

No answer. Seconds later she called again. No answer. The volume on the television suddenly increased.

The husband called, "Christine! Turn off the TV and come in here. Now!"

The volume increased again. "Excuse me," the mother said and walked from the room. Seconds later the TV set stopped and seven-year-old Christine came in, being pushed by her mother.

"You heard your mother and me yelling at you, Christine!" the irate father said.

For a moment she played the silence game, lowered her head and stared at her feet. Then she said, "But

124

Daddy, you know I can't hear you when I'm not listening!" The story of Christine reminds me of the way many of us live today. We can't hear. We're not listening.

I'm a preacher of the gospel. Week after week I study, doing my best to hear from God and to be the divine medium. I like to think that many times the Holy Spirit speaks through me. But at times it seems fruitless. Disheartening. People listen all right. At least they hear the words, the sound of my voice. But I wonder how deeply the message penetrates. I wonder how many times they don't hear because they're not listening.

I'm not the only preacher who feels this way. I suppose most preachers and teachers do. We try. We give our best. But sometimes we wonder if it's worth the effort.

Jesus knew the human situation. Many times he spoke a parable. A simple story about two men who built houses in Palestine. One built well, the other poorly. One house stood, the other fell. Jesus said, "The one who hears and obeys builds upon a solid foundation. The one who hears but lacks follow-through is like a person building a house upon sand."

We all know that. Many of us as tiny tots waved hands up and down as we sang, "The wise man built his house upon the rock." We knew the words so well. But we haven't always listened to what the words tell us. Hearing the Word of God is important. Anyone who wants spiritual growth finds much of it through hearing and reading the Bible.

Yet I've heard every conceivable excuse as to why people don't come to church or why they don't read their Bibles. That doesn't mean there aren't honest reasons—sickness, inaccessibility, emergencies.

But I get concerned about purposely not hearing

125

what God says. "You know I can't hear you when I'm not listening."

The transparency of faces often amazes me as I stand behind a pulpit or in a classroom. Bored stares. Some stifle yawns. Others gaze at the architecture. I see faces with a sign that says, "closed until noon." Or sleepy eyes. Or indifference looking around at bald heads or curly mustaches.

But I also thank God that I often see alertness. Excitement. Openness. This second group gives us a sense of encouragement and the realization that something does take place.

Jesus says he acknowledges the person who hears *and* obeys. But we have to hear first. And hearing implies reading, thinking, studying, grasping, understanding. Jesus primarily taught an uneducated, illiterate people. He used the medium they could grasp— the verbal presentation. But he implied more. How can we do God's will unless we know it? How can we obey unless we're listening?

One of the saddest periods in the history of Israel is contained in the Book of Judges. Over and over a single phrase occurs: "Every man did what was right in his own eyes." It was a time of spiritual anarchy. There was no king, no charismatic leader like Moses or Joshua on the scene. Isaiah, Jeremiah and Daniel were yet centuries away. A few minor leaders rose up from time to time. All weak, imperfect beings. None of the "judges" was able to maintain moral discipline and spiritual vigor in Israel for more than a short period of time.

Then Samson came along—divinely promised, specially endowed with physical strength. But his possibilities were wasted through ignorance or selfish lust. True religion and faithful teaching had been lost. How could the people hear what God said?

Later, in the days of King Josiah, someone accidentally found a biblical scroll. The Jews had been without the Sacred Word for years. A prophet brought the scroll to King Josiah. He read it and God's spirit convicted him of his faithlessness. The scroll was then read to the people. A revival took place. The people heard what God was saying. Obedience led to repentance, to changing directions.

None of us can know the will of God until we first listen to him. We have to be in the places where God speaks! I don't think God's voice is heard too clearly on Sunday morning on the seventh hole. Or under an electric blanket at 11:12 A.M.

Listening for God implies being physically present where he speaks. Part of the result of staying away from church is a gross ignorance of the Bible. But preachers and teachers can fail to listen as well as those who occupy the pews.

A dark-haired Bible college senior sat next to me in a sharing group. We went around a circle quoting our favorite Bible verse. My first shock: so few could actually quote a single verse! And their favorite, too! The second shock followed immediately: the Bible college senior said, "My favorite Bible verse, and one that always gives me such comfort is: 'Only one life, 'twill soon be past; only what's done for Christ will last.'"

Her ignorance really wasn't much worse than that of the ordained minister who said to me one evening, "The Scripture that has helped me most through dark places is the one that says, 'God works in mysterious ways His wonders to perform.'"

Shocked, I blurted out, "I think Cowper wrote that."

"No, no, it's in the Bible. I'm sure I've read it there. In Isaiah, I think. Or maybe it's Jeremiah."

How can we obey if we don't hear? How can we hear if we won't listen? We may reply that preaching is dull

127

or like summer TV—nothing but reruns of reruns. We've "heard" the gospel too often and too long. But have we heard enough that it stimulates us to obey? Do we listen—really listen—so that we know what God wants? And once we know His will, do we carry it out?

Or are too many of us like Christine? "God, you know I can't hear you when I'm not listening."

Listen. That's where I'm struggling in my own relationship with Jesus Christ. I want to live a joyous, fulfilling life. And this life is available only in Jesus Christ. By hearing and by obeying, I can strive to live a Christian life!

DATE DUE

GAYLORD